The Vine Speaks

Dear Suzanne,

God's rich blessings in Christ, the Vine.

Love,
Cindy

The Vine Speaks

Eleven Lessons from John 15
A Women's Small-Group Bible Study

Cindy STEINBECK

CONCORDIA PUBLISHING HOUSE · SAINT LOUIS

Published by Concordia Publishing House
3558 S. Jefferson Avenue, St. Louis, MO 63118-3968
1-800-325-3040 · www.cph.org

Manufactured in the United States of America

1 2 3 4 5 6 7 8 9 10   22 21 20 19 18 17 16 15 14 13

Thank you, my dear family, Mom, Dad, Ryan, Caitlin, Bradley, Stacy, and Bryan, for traveling with me on this writing journey. Thank you, Julie and Cecilia, my cherished journeying friends. Joanne and Allen, thank you for proofreading my work and offering loving guidance. Leslie, thank you for your artistry that helped make The Vine speak clearly.

Table of Contents

The Vine Speaks!

A grapevine cannot talk as humans do, but it can speak. Three hundred thousand grapevines in our family's vineyard have spoken to me. I am at home on the soil, among the vines. My faith has grown by watching our vines grow. My faith and understanding of it have grown by watching the work my father does and by observing the work our employees accomplish. And I've grown by working on and among the vines.

I am continuously learning what it means to be at home and to grow as a branch in The Vine—Christ Jesus. Here in the pages of *The Vine Speaks,* I share some of the truths I've discovered among the grapevines and some of the details of my journey in the life of The Vine. For me, being at home and growing in Christ, The Vine, means welcoming growth in my heart, mind, and life. Growth is not easy because it usually means change, and change is hard—but growth is the way of life in The Vine. I invite you to see through my eyes what Jesus may have meant in John 15:5 when He declared Himself "the vine" and us "the branches."

The Vine Speaks is a conversational Bible study springing from Jesus' words "I am the vine; you are the branches." Each chapter begins with the heading "The Vine Speaks: My Father's Vineyard." In this section, I offer my understanding of grapevines and the vineyard as it relates to this Bible passage. I did not study viticulture in college, but I've worked among the vines long enough to pick up on vineyard practices. Please imagine a tour with me through my vineyard and process with me my observations. Smell the soil, watch the growth, taste the fruit, and observe the seasonal changes.

Each chapter includes a section called "The Vine Speaks: Jesus' Words." Christ, The Vine, speaks! Jesus' words from the Gospels fill this section and give us opportunity to dig into them. You will notice that I regularly place the words "word and work" together. I believe that The Vine's word and work accomplished all that He promised then and promises now. His word and work cannot be separated; they bring growth and life and healing and hope.

Every chapter also includes a section titled "The Branches Speak: The Apostles' Words." The branches of The Vine, His apostles, heard and saw and believed. Having heard and seen and believed, they followed Jesus' call to speak His word and work His work. As branches of The Vine, the apostles bore fruit through their words and works, helping us dig into the rich meaning of Jesus' words "I am the vine; you are the branches."

Some chapters include a section titled "The Vinedresser Speaks: God's Word from the Old Testament." Jesus said, "I am the true vine and My Father is the vinedresser." We dig into the rich meaning through the words of God, The Vinedresser, in the Old Testament. Christ, The Vine's word and work, took root before the foundations of the world. God, The Vinedresser, speaks through the Old Testament with important messages in this study.

Each chapter concludes with the sections "The Branches Speak: My Story" and "The Branches Speak: Your Story." The branches of a healthy vine grow and produce fruit. I pray that my story will give you courage to embrace growth and discover your story as a branch of The Vine. I also pray that you will be called to identify the fruit you have produced and the fruit God is calling you to produce. To that end, I have included thought-provoking questions for you to consider as you read each chapter. Small-group Bible study and discussion are encouraged, although *The Vine Speaks* can be used for personal study as well.

As the fruit of my work on this book unfolded, I began to see two options for small-group study. Your group may choose to use this Bible study by walking through it from cover to cover. Or, your group might rather choose to study and discuss only one section of each chapter. For example, your group could study each chapter's vineyard examples along with "The Vine Speaks: Jesus' Words."

Whichever option you choose, I pray that The Vine speaks to you! God bless your journey into the life of The Vine!

The Author

Chapter One

THE VINE

THE VINE SPEAKS: MY FATHER'S VINEYARD

A grapevine speaks, but it cannot talk. The vines speak to me as I live and work in my father's vineyard in Paso Robles, California. (I own the vineyard, too, but to me it sounds better when I call it "my father's vineyard.")

In 1997, the vines called me home from a professional ministry career as a director of Christian education. The Vine, Christ Jesus, calls each of us to be at home in Him today in a rich, alive, growing sense. My hope is that this magnificent plant God created, the grapevine, will speak to you as it does to me. I pray that God will work through my understanding of the vine so that The Vine speaks to you as you read this book.

Vineyard practices vary, but there are some basic, common practices that provide the springboard for our study:

- Grapevines need soil in which to be planted, water, and nutrients.

- Grapevines need to be trained, pruned, and thinned. There are challenges a grower of vines faces, and if a vine isn't growing, there are problems that need to be addressed.

- Grapevines have a basic structure, including the root system, which is entirely underground.

- They have a trunk that was once a supple branch and has been trained up and remains for the life of the vine.

- Vines in a vineyard have a graft union into which the varietal was grafted.

- Vines contain branches, tendrils, leaves, buds, and fruit.

- The goal of growing grapevines is fruit production, which in my family's business is crafted into premium dry wine.

The following sketched diagrams help define terms associated with growing grapes and give a foundation for Jesus' words "I am the vine; you are the branches." This is not a technical manual on the physiology of the grapevine; it is a work about the heart of Jesus, The Vine, and His call to grow in Him from the context of the vine.

Grapevines are stunningly beautiful, but it seems to me that everyone who comes to our vineyard for wine tasting is drawn to the vine on a far deeper level than its exterior beauty. Guests love our dusty, bumpy vineyard Jeep tour. They love hearing about the work going on in the field at any given time, and they are fascinated that grapevines need so much care and so many hands-on touches in order to produce premium fruit. After an in-depth look at the vine, guests at my father's vineyard have a far greater appreciation for a glass of wine.

Grapevines grow and bear fruit for thirty to fifty years. Every year in the life of the vine is intimately connected to previous and future years. A microscopic look at a cross section of a bud prior to bud break reveals this wonder. All of the coming year's growth, including the leaves and fruit, is tightly wound up inside the bud. Tiny buds grew on a shoot last year,

Pruned Vine

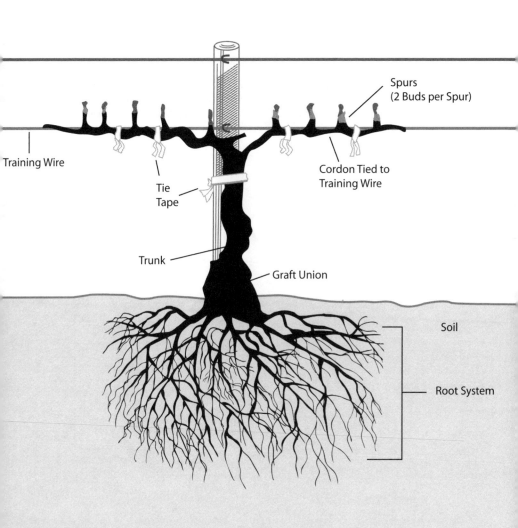

Training Wire

Tie
Tape

Trunk

Graft Union

Spurs
(2 Buds per Spur)

Cordon Tied to
Training Wire

Soil

Root System

Mature Vine

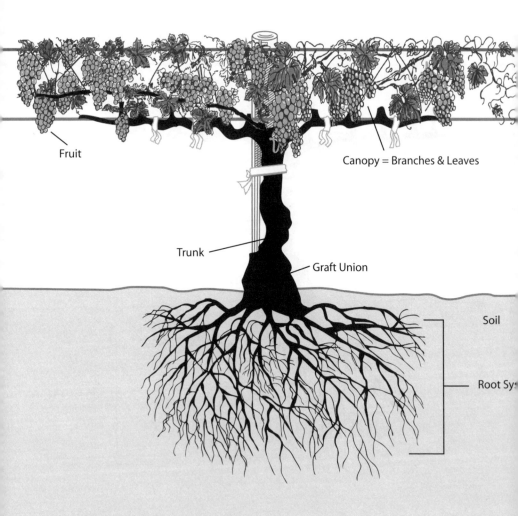

Fruit

Canopy = Branches & Leaves

Trunk

Graft Union

Soil

Root Sys

which was grown on wood from the previous year. Every year in the life of the vine is connected to the past and to the future.

Another foundational principle of growing vines—or any other type of farming, for that matter—is sustainability. The soil and other natural resources are magnificent gifts from our Creator. God provides, and we use the gifts wisely. We love the land, and we take great care to sustain it. We know that it provides our livelihood and our lifestyle. Every decision we make takes into account safety for our families, workers, and the community; every action must be economically sustainable so the next generations can also live off the land.

These two examples—of the present bud connected to both the past and the future and of the soil, which must be sustained—provide rich analogies for our study. Take the first example deeper: the present moment in our lives is intimately connected to our past as well as to our future. God's Word calls us to live fully and grow continually in the present while honoring our past and anticipating His work for our future. He calls us to trust that His work in our lives brings forth growth and fruit.

The second example leads us to confess that life is truly sustainable only in and through Christ, The Vine. Sustainability means stewardship of the gifts we've been given—the soil and natural resources, the environment, and the future of our land and families. In the richest sense of the word, sustainability in The Vine means living and dwelling in Christ in the present and for eternity. Life is truly sustainable in The Vine.

THE VINEDRESSER SPEAKS:
GOD'S WORD FROM THE OLD TESTAMENT

Every moment of God's work is intimately connected to His past work and to His future work. Jesus said, "I am the true vine and My Father is the vinedresser." A vinedresser is a master gardener, one who oversees the vines and makes decisions for the health and growth of a vine. A later chapter is devoted to The Vinedresser. But for now, ponder these words of introduction from the Old Testament, The Vinedresser's words about a vine. (As you do, note that the vine speaking is not a new concept!) These verses are a fascinating account of God speaking in parable form to get the children of Israel to wake up to the evil that Abimelech had committed against his family and Israel. Olive trees and a grapevine shared this conversation about the crowning of the new, evil king:

> And the trees said to the vine, "You come and reign over us." But *the vine said to them,* "Shall I leave my wine that cheers God and men and go hold sway over the trees?" Then all the trees said to the bramble, "You come and reign over us." And the bramble said to the trees, "If in good faith you are anointing me king over you, then come and take refuge in my shade, but if not, let fire come out of the bramble and devour the cedars of Lebanon." (Judges 9:12–15, emphasis added)

The imagery of the vine was spoken by almost every author of the Old Testament. Through the prophets, God spoke punishment through the vine. One form of punishment He rained down on the people was that they would plant a vineyard but not enjoy the fruit or the wine from it. Ouch! That was serious punishment.

God also promised deliverance using vineyard imagery. The Vine-dresser said, "They shall plant vineyards and eat their fruit" (Isaiah 65:21). And a beautiful promise using the vine imagery comes through the psalmist's words as he declared that God brought a vine out of Egypt and planted it:

> You brought a *vine out of Egypt;* You drove out the nations and planted it. You cleared the ground for it; *it took deep root and filled the land.* The mountains were covered with its shade, the mighty cedars with its branches. It sent out its branches to the sea and its shoots to the River. Why then have You broken down its walls, so that all who pass along the way pluck its fruit? The boar from the forest ravages it, and all that move in the field feed on it.
>
> Turn again, O God of hosts! Look down from heaven, and see; *have regard for this vine, the stock that Your right hand planted, and for the son whom You made strong for Yourself.* They have burned it with fire; they have cut it down; may they perish at the rebuke of Your face! But let Your hand be on the man of Your right hand, the son of man whom You have made strong for Yourself! Then we shall not turn back from You; give us life, and we will call upon Your name!
>
> Restore us, O LORD God of hosts! Let Your face shine, that we may be saved! (Psalm 80:8–19, emphasis added)

Jesus is The Vine that God brought up out of Egypt. He was planted. He was ravaged. God had regard for the stock He planted with His right hand and made His Son strong for His purpose—life and salvation in and through The Vine. The Vinedresser desires that we know His heart and grow according to the work of His hands. The Vine speaks to us today, calling us to allow The Vinedresser's work, which is to grow and bear mature fruit in Him.

The Vine Speaks: Jesus' Words

I am the true vine, and My Father is the vinedresser. Every branch in Me that does not bear fruit He takes away, and every branch that does bear fruit He prunes, that it may bear more fruit. Already you are clean because of the word that I have spoken to you. Abide in Me, and I in you. As the branch cannot bear fruit by itself, unless it abides in the vine, neither can you, unless you abide in Me. I am the vine; you are the branches. Whoever abides in Me and I in him, he it is that bears much fruit, for apart from Me you can do nothing. (John 15:1–5)

Jesus' words "I am the vine" would have resonated with those of Jewish heritage, who had heard the punishments and promises using vine imagery. What may have been new to them was Jesus' declaration that God was The Vinedresser! That was a job only for poor peasants (more in chapter 5). Jesus spoke the words "I am the vine" just before He left the Upper Room to face the cross. These words are the context from which He calls His followers to abide in Him, to keep His commands, to ask anything in His name, and to bear fruit that will last.

I have read and listened to Jesus' words many times. Each time, something new touches my heart and calls my attention to how God wants me to grow. Read John 15:1-17 aloud a few times. Underline the verses that stand out in your mind, and discuss them with your group:

> I am the true vine, and My Father is the vinedresser. Every branch in Me that does not bear fruit He takes away, and every branch that does bear fruit He prunes, that it may bear more fruit. Already you are clean because of the word that I have spoken to you. Abide in Me, and I in you. As the branch cannot bear fruit by itself, unless it abides in the vine, neither can you, unless you abide in Me. I am the vine; you are the branches. Whoever abides in Me and I in him, he it is that bears much fruit, for apart from Me you can do nothing. If anyone does not abide in Me he is thrown away like a branch and withers; and the branches are gathered, thrown into the fire, and burned. If you abide in Me, and My words abide in you, ask whatever you wish, and it will be done for you. By this My Father is glorified, that you bear much fruit and so prove to be My disciples. As the Father has loved Me, so have I loved you. Abide in My love. If you keep My commandments, you will abide in My love, just as I have kept My Father's commandments and abide in His love. These things I have spoken to you, that My joy may be in you, and that your joy may be full.

> This is My commandment, that you love one another as I have loved you. Greater love has no one than this, that someone lay down his life for his friends. You are My friends if you do what I command you. No longer do I call you servants, for the servant does not know what his master is doing; but I have called you friends, for all that I have

heard from My Father I have made known to you. You did not choose Me, but I chose you and appointed you that you should go and bear fruit and that your fruit should abide, so that whatever you ask the Father in My name, He may give it to you. These things I command you, so that you will love one another. (John 15:1–17)

The diagrams on pages 15–16 show the various parts of the vine and the branches. I propose for this study that we read the first six verses of John 15 as if Jesus spoke about the vine and the branches in two different but closely related ways. Discussing pruning and thinning (John 15:2–3) requires us to look at the branches as the part of the vine that grows leaves and bears fruit. On the trellis system in my vineyard, the cordon is tied to the wire and remains there from year to year. The branches push out from the buds on the spurs of the cordon ("Pruned Vine," p. 15).

In John 15:5–6, Jesus' words "I am the vine; you are the branches" require a slightly different understanding of a branch in the vine. We, the branches in The Vine, grow from the graft union up. The branch is all of the plant above the graft union, including the trunk. The vine begins below the graft union and includes the trunk into which the bud is grafted and the root system. These two distinctions of the word *branch* will help us understand Jesus' words.

THE BRANCHES SPEAK: THE APOSTLES' WORDS

The apostles were and are living branches in The Vine. The apostles heard The Vine speak, and having heard, they spoke. Today, we enjoy the fruit of their speaking. The apostles witnessed The Vine's work, and so they witnessed to others about it. Today, we enjoy the fruit of their witness. They believed that The Vine's word and His work brought growth and fruit, and we believe that happens today by the same word and work.

When Jesus said "I am the vine; you are the branches," the apostles may have pondered their relationship with Him. They may have wished that He just spoke plainly. I imagine them doing the same when He said, "I am He" in response to the religious leaders' harsh judgment of Him or "I am the resurrection and the life" at the tomb of their dead friend or "I am the way, and the truth, and the life" in reply to Thomas's question about where Jesus was going (John 11:25; 14:6).

Their thoughts may have turned to their last vineyard experience with Jesus and the words He said to them then. In my experience, we listen differently if we are in the field, standing among the vines, than we do when we are sitting in a conference room or at a kitchen table. John recorded these words from Jesus' teaching in the Upper Room, but what did The Vine speak among the vines? John also says that many more things could have been written, but that he wrote these that we might believe and, in believing, have life in Jesus' name (John 20:30–31).

John focused on the word *abide,* or *dwell,* and quotes Jesus speaking this word seven times in these few verses. I am astounded that John wrote his Gospel fifty years after Jesus spoke the words "abide in Me." His words are crisp and fresh and clear today as he draws us into Jesus' abiding relationship to God. He speaks it in the very first chapter of his Gospel as he proclaims God in human form choosing to dwell among us. John continued drawing attention to the words *abide* and *dwell* throughout his Gospel. His letters provide further insight:

> Let what you heard from the beginning *abide* in you. If what you heard from the beginning *abides in you,* then you too will *abide in the Son and in the Father.* And this is the promise that He made to us—eternal life.
>
> I write these things to you about those who are trying to

deceive you. But the anointing that you received from *Him abides in you,* and you have no need that anyone should teach you. But as His anointing teaches you about everything, and is true, and is no lie—just as it has taught you, *abide in Him.*

And now, little children, *abide in Him,* so that when He appears we may have confidence and not shrink from Him in shame at His coming. (1 John 2:24–28, emphasis added)

Paul used the imagery of the olive tree when he spoke about grafting, but the same grafting practices are used for grapevines. Paul could have been contemplating grafting when he wrote the words "in Christ" in his letters. As I search, I find that Paul used the words "in Christ" ninety times! I believe he was talking about the flesh-on-flesh relationship we have with Christ and with one another in Christ. Paul's words about grafting in Romans 11, which we will discuss in the following chapter, led to powerful words about being in Christ:

For by the grace given to me I say to everyone among you not to think of himself more highly than he ought to think, but to think with sober judgment, each according to the measure of faith that God has assigned. For as in one body we have many members, and the members do not all have the same function, so we, though many, are *one body in Christ,* and individually members one of another. (Romans 12:3–5, emphasis added)

As a biblical concept, the word *dwell* is rich in meaning for this study of the relationship of the vine and the branches. In the Old Testament, God chose to dwell among people in various forms, including a bush, a cloud, a pillar of fire, and on the ark of the covenant. In the New Testament, the abiding relationship between God and man took on new form as the Word, who was with God from the beginning and came to dwell physically among us.

The Word created all things; the Word became flesh and dwelt among us; the Word proclaimed, "I am the vine." John proceeds in his proclamation of the Word made flesh, recording Jesus' words: "I am in the Father and the Father is in Me" and "you are in Me and I am in you." The branches of The Vine communicated His very heart: He dwells among us, He dwells in us, and we are grafted into His life.

THE BRANCHES SPEAK: MY STORY

My father's first grapevines were planted in the winter of 1982. I remember the yearling vines and the excitement of my parents' venture at the newly named Steinbeck Vineyards. The ranch I had grown up on was a cattle and barley operation with wide-open spaces. I grew up building forts, hunting, and playing in the soil. I was accustomed to watching glorious sunrises and sunsets from the porches of our home. I slept outside under the stars every summer and protested being told to sleep inside when school started in September.

Mom and Dad began the transition to vineyards when I was away at college in Portland, Oregon. The tiny vines surrounded the family home and were a spectacular sight of green growth amid the brown Paso Robles hillsides. Each of the thirty thousand plants was lovingly and tediously watered by hand in those early days; Dad didn't build the irrigation system until after the vines were planted.

I've experienced our vines in many different ways. I've seen them from airplanes at twenty-five thousand and seven thousand feet. I see them from the windows and porches of my home. I've seen the vines up close as I've worked to prune or train them. I've driven a tractor through every acre of the vines many times. And I've seen my vines from the ground up, while lying on my back as I slowly regained consciousness after crashing my four-wheeled ATV.

I placed my burdens among the vines in Row 124, as you'll learn about as my story unfolds. I know that the vines and the soil they are rooted in can absorb my brokenness. Just as Jesus said He could—and He does. (You're welcome to come tour my vineyard and also place your burdens among the vines in Row 124, if you'd like.)

The young vines I stood among for my wedding photos are now aged and rough after years of growth. They are beautiful nevertheless, and today they produce incredible, mature fruit.

But unlike those vines, my marriage didn't mature. It didn't grow in intimacy or beauty, only in pain and deep brokenness, and so it has ended. The vines spoke to me, calling me to live during the darkest times. They spoke life and healing and growth as I journeyed through the perils of an unhealthy relationship and divorce. I wanted a beautiful ending to my story, and God will work that, but not in the way I expected or dreamed about. My story and yours are different, but I know and you know that Jesus, The Vine, knows our brokenness.

Row 55 is another row you'll read about later. I call it "Eternity Row" because it is a row for rejoicing in the many blessings God has given. It has also been a place to ponder Paul's call to give thanks *in* all circumstances (not *for* all circumstances). Row 55 has been a place for me to practice thanksgiving and trusting, and it has been a place for growing.

The Vine speaks healing and growing and calls us to bear fruit through our stories. Jesus abides in us, and we abide in Him and His holy life, no matter where we live. We live in Christ now and for eternity. That is what *The Vine Speaks!*

I know how easy it is to look over my vineyard and believe everything to be perfect and beautiful. My father knows differently because he sees the vines from a vinedresser's perspective. He sees the challenges and problems. He sees the work that needs to be done. It is also easy to believe everyone else's life to be without challenges. It is easy to judge how others grow their vines and grow in their lives and then to withdraw or isolate ourselves because we don't see ourselves as perfect and beautiful. But neither withdrawing nor judging is the way of life in The Vine. We are His branches, and we do what healthy branches of The True Vine do: we listen to Him speak, we receive His nourishment, and then we respond in faith, we grow, and we bear fruit.

THE BRANCHES SPEAK: YOUR STORY

Contemplating the words in this book during personal, private time will bring growth and fruit. Gathering in small groups as the branches of The Vine is also a wonderful way to ponder and study this book. As you gather with your small group, promise one another that as growing branches, you will cherish one another and keep in confidence what the group members speak.

Please discuss these questions:

1. What has The Vine spoken to you in this chapter?
2. What burdens would you choose to leave in Row 124 in the soil at the foot of The Vine?
3. What rejoicing would you like to do in Row 55?
4. Share a time when The Vine or The Vinedresser or the branches of the Vine spoke through the Scriptures to you.

Chapter Two

GRAFTED INTO THE VINE

THE VINE SPEAKS: MY FATHER'S VINEYARD

Each of the 300,000 grapevines in my father's five-hundred-acre vineyard grows slightly crooked from a point just above the soil. This is because the grape varietal was grafted into the root—or as we call it, rootstock—at that point. Each grapevine begins its life as two separate plants in the nursery. One plant is the rootstock, a vine that grows but doesn't produce fruit. Rootstock is developed and propagated at nurseries. It provides a host home for the type of grape, or varietal, we specify. The other plant is the varietal (such as Cabernet Sauvignon), from which buds are cut and grafted into the rootstock. Nurseries provide many choices of rootstock, which are selected for soil, rainfall, climate, and the vigor of the plant desired. Rootstock is not susceptible to the diseases and pests that attack a vine grown on its own root.

Grafting is very precise work and is left to the experts. Nurseries make recommendations based on a particular vineyard's soil and climate and then propagate the vines according to the vineyard's specific requests. Specialists cut a deep, V-shaped slice into the flesh of the rootstock just

Graft Union

above the soil level. A tiny bud from the varietal is cut to match the slice in the rootstock. The bud is placed into the flesh of the rootstock, and a Band-Aid-like tape is placed over the wound with just the tip of the bud left uncovered. The vine and the bud "bleed" and grow together to form one grapevine.

The graft union of rootstock and bud heals within a couple of weeks. Within a year, the graft union is strong. The tiny Cabernet bud pushes and grows. Once established, the experts cut away the rootstock growth just above the graft union. The tiny plant, once two different plants, is now one plant made up of the rootstock and the varietal. The tiny grafted vines are planted in the freshly prepared soil. After much training, the first crop of grapes is harvested three years later. These vines produce fruit annually for thirty to fifty years.

The graft union grows as the plants grow, but the healed scar can always be seen, just above the soil. Guests in my vineyard are fascinated when I point out the graft union on every vine and how every vine grows slightly crooked. The 300,000 grapevines in our vineyard grow on rootstock that is not susceptible to the disease and pests that attack a vine growing on its original root system.

THE VINE SPEAKS: JESUS' WORDS

I am the true vine, and My Father is the vinedresser. Every branch in Me that does not bear fruit He takes away, and every branch that does bear fruit He prunes, that it may bear more fruit. Already you are clean because of the word that I have spoken to you. Abide in Me, and I in you. As the branch cannot bear fruit by itself, unless it abides in the vine, neither can you, unless you abide in Me. I am the vine; you are the branches. Whoever abides in Me and I in him, he it is that bears much fruit, for apart from Me you can do nothing. (John 15:1–5)

Jesus, The Vine, is our rootstock. We were grafted into His holy life in Baptism or when we came to faith in Him. Jesus, our rootstock, is not susceptible to disease or death or sin. In Holy Baptism or when we came to faith in Jesus, we were cut away from the old and placed into a new dwelling or abiding place.

We were cut away from our old life and grafted into His holy life not of our own doing, but by the hands of the expert grafter—God, The Vinedresser. We are that tiny little bud, cut away from our old self and placed into His life by Him. He bled, we bleed, and our lives form one flesh. We become a branch in The Vine. He is The Vine, which includes the root system; we are the branches from the graft union up. We are fully alive in His life, growing and bearing fruit according to His will.

Jesus, our rootstock, was born into this world to dwell among us. Jesus lived a perfect life; He was tempted in every way that we are, and still He did not sin. Jesus spoke mercy and healing as He walked this earth. Jesus, our rootstock, suffered and died and rose to life. Our lives are grafted into His perfect life. Our living place, dwelling place, abiding place is Christ's life.

Jesus proclaimed, "I am the vine; you are the branches. Abide in Me." To "abide" means to dwell, remain, stay. It also means to continue in an attitude or particular condition. *Abide* is a rich, active word that John chose to use nine times in his Gospel and eighteen times in his letters. John begs us to clearly see Jesus' call on our lives, the call into a living, growing relationship in and with The Vine. Jesus calls us to see that abiding in Him is a continuous action that He works and accomplishes.

The tiny little bud grows and becomes a branch that dwells *in* the vine. The Vine calls our attention to another fact of the relationship between the rootstock and the tiny bud: Jesus, The Vine, dwells in us. He dwells in us *and* we dwell in Him. We live in Christ; Christ lives in us. We live our lives, now and eternally, in His life, His resurrected life. His aliveness is alive in us.

He works the miracle of life in us as He dwells in us by His word and work; He works life in us by His word and work as we dwell in Him. Jesus' word and work are two aspects of the same life-giving life! Our life is alive in Him, grafted into His life. He calls us to see that life is about living, being, growing, and thriving in His aliveness. He calls us to see the even bigger picture that even our physical dying is living fully alive in His life. "In Christ," it doesn't matter where "here" is.

Jesus' words come to life as we picture Him as our rootstock and our lives grafted into The Vine. I highlight the word *abide* because I believe that being grafted into Jesus' life is what Jesus was conveying. The Vine says:

- Abide in Me, and I in you. As the branch cannot bear fruit by itself, unless it abides in the vine, neither can you, unless you abide in Me. I am the vine; you are the branches. Whoever abides in Me and I in him, he it is that bears much fruit, for apart from Me you can do nothing. (John 15:4–5)

- If you abide in Me, and My words abide in you, ask whatever you wish, and it will be done for you. (John 15:7)

- As the Father has loved Me, so have I loved you. Abide in My love. (John 15:9)

35

The grafted bud abides in the vine and becomes part of the vine, growing into a fruit-producing branch. We abide in Christ; we have been grafted into Him through Baptism. The scar from the graft is a vivid reminder of the relationship we share with The Vine: we bled when we were cut away; He bled as we were grafted into Him. The wound healed, and the visible scar is a reminder of the healing.

The Vine's words take on even more depth and beauty as we dig into the words He spoke about His abiding, dwelling relationship with His Father and His abiding, dwelling relationship with us. Also note Jesus' use of the words "word and work" as one and the same:

- Philip said to Him, "Lord, show us the Father, and it is enough for us." Jesus said to him, "Have I been with you so long, and you still do not know Me, Philip? Whoever has seen Me has seen the Father. How can you say, 'Show us the Father'? *Do you not believe that I am in the Father and the Father is in Me?* The *words* that I say to you I do not speak on My own authority, but *the Father who dwells in Me does His works.* (John 14:8–10, emphasis added)

- I will not leave you as orphans; I will come to you. Yet a little while and the world will see Me no more, but you will see Me. Because I live, you also will live. In that day *you will know that I am in My Father, and you in Me, and I in you.* (John 14:18–20, emphasis added)

The flesh-on-flesh relationship of the vine and the branches helps us understand the relationships between

- the Father, Son, and Holy Spirit;

- us and the triune God; and

- the triune God and us.

For now, we will focus on the abiding relationships of the triune God to us and us to Him. Later we will discuss the relationship between dwelling in Christ, keeping His commands, and bearing fruit.

The Vine speaks! When He speaks, He calls us to understand the work He has already accomplished for us and in us and the work He continues to work. The Vine says, "You abide, dwell, and live in My life; I abide, dwell, and live in you." It was His word and work in us that established the relationship, not our own work. And His word and work act continuously in the relationship as The Vine and the branches grow and bear fruit.

The Branches Speak: The Apostles' Words

The Vine speaks, and the branches speak in response to the life The Vine works in them. The apostles grew up in The Vine, and their words bear lasting fruit for Him. The apostles speak to us from the context of life in The Vine from their heart of hearts, from deep within their soul. They experienced the living Lord, and they want us to journey into a deeper relationship with Him through their words. John, Peter, and Paul are the branches of the vine I've chosen to highlight here, through the lens of Jesus' words "I am the vine." The branches' heart is revealed through their letters as they call us to believe and trust the relationship Christ began as He grafted us into His life—to trust Christ as He calls us to grow and bear fruit. I ask that you focus on the words of relationship in Christ, The Vine, as the branches speak. You will notice the branches using language such as "keep," "love," and "walk." In later chapters, we will pay attention to the keeping as He kept, the loving as He loved, and the walking as He walked. For now, though, we will concentrate on being grafted in Christ.

The apostle John followed Jesus at His call, and as he followed, he watched Him heal people and calm storms with His words. John listened to Jesus, the Son of God, speak the truth in the midst of fiery religious turmoil as He accomplished His word and work. John watched Jesus suffer and cry out, "God, why have You forsaken Me?" John witnessed Jesus' death. John saw the risen Jesus overcome that death. And John received Jesus' words: *"Peace be with you."*

Meditate on these words from John's letters:

- Whoever says "I know Him" but does not keep His commandments is a liar, and the truth is not in him, but whoever keeps His word, in him truly the love of God is perfected. By this *we may know that we are in Him:* whoever says he *abides in Him* ought to walk in the same way in which He walked. (1 John 2:4–6, emphasis added)

- *Let what you heard from the beginning abide in you.* If what you heard from the beginning abides in you, then *you too will abide in the Son and in the Father.* And this is the promise that He made to us—eternal life. (1 John 2:24–25, emphasis added)

- And this is His commandment, that we believe in the name of His Son Jesus Christ and love one another, just as He has commanded us. Whoever keeps His commandments *abides in God, and God in him.* And by this we know that He *abides in us, by the Spirit whom He has given us.* (1 John 3:23–24, emphasis added)

- By this we know that we *abide in Him and He in us,* because He has given us of His Spirit. And we have seen and testify that the Father has sent His Son to be the Savior of the world. Whoever confesses that Jesus is the Son of God, *God abides in him, and he in God.* So we have come to know and to believe the love that God has for us. *God is love, and whoever abides in love abides in God, and God abides in him.* (1 John 4:13–16, emphasis added)

- And we know that the Son of God has come and has given us understanding, so that we may know Him who is true; and *we are in Him who is true, in His Son Jesus Christ.* He is the true God and eternal life. Little children, keep yourselves from idols. (1 John 5:20–21)

The apostle Peter dropped his fishing net and followed Jesus' call. He confessed Christ as Lord and shortly thereafter tried to convince Jesus to turn away from the cross. Peter said, "No You will not wash my feet" and "Wash all of me," falling short of Jesus' desire for relationship with him in both statements. Peter confidently told Jesus he would follow Him unto death. He vehemently denied knowing Jesus to a young servant girl. But Peter died proclaiming Christ. Luke records,

Then Peter, filled with the Holy Spirit, said to them, "Rulers of the people and elders, if we are being examined today concerning a good deed done to a crippled man, by what means this man has been healed, let it be known to all of you and to all the people of Israel that by the name of Jesus Christ of Nazareth, whom you crucified, whom God raised from the dead—by Him this man is standing before you well. This Jesus is the stone that was rejected by you, the builders, which has become the cornerstone. And there is salvation in no one else, for there is no other name under heaven given among men by which we must be saved." Now when they saw the boldness of Peter and John, and perceived that they were uneducated, common men, they were astonished. And they recognized that they had been with Jesus. (Acts 4:8–13)

Salvation and life and healing are found in Christ alone. Peter confessed Christ and called people into relationship with and in the living

Christ until he breathed his last breath. Peter proclaimed these verses (my favorite verses): "He himself bore our sins in His body on the tree, that we might die to sin and live to righteousness. By His wounds you have been healed. For you were straying like sheep, but have now returned to the Shepherd and Overseer of your souls" (1 Peter 2:24–25).

Note that Peter spoke in past tense when he declared, "By His wounds you have been healed." The healing has already taken place; we are called to learn what that means for us right here, right now. Visualize the graft wound on the vine and the tiny bud placed into the wound. Picture the Band-Aid firmly holding the two together as they bleed and the wound forms a scab. The wound heals and forms one flesh. The scar grows as the trunk of the vine grows. The graft union on each vine is a visual reminder of Christ's wounds and our healing in His wounds.

Saul passionately pursued religious purity and worked to purge the world of the movement to follow the Son of God. The risen Christ confronted him on his journey toward Damascus (where Saul was planning to wipe out more of Jesus' followers) with the words "Saul, Saul, why are you persecuting Me?" Christ grafted Saul into His life, changing his life and his mission. Saul (later called Paul) powerfully proclaimed life in Christ then and now, calling us to grow in Him, in faith, and in our understanding of life in Christ. Pay particular attention to Paul's words, "*in Christ.*" The flesh-on-flesh relationship *in Christ* is our dwelling place:

- Do you not know that all of us who have been *baptized into Christ Jesus* were baptized into His death? We were buried therefore with Him by Baptism into death, in order that, just as Christ was raised from the dead by the glory of the Father, we too might walk in newness of life. (Romans 6:3–4, emphasis added)

- There is therefore now *no condemnation for those who are in*

Christ Jesus. For the law of the *Spirit of life has set you free in Christ Jesus* from the law of sin and death. (Romans 8:1–2, emphasis added)

- Now if we have died with Christ, we believe that we will also live with Him. We know that Christ, being raised from the dead, will never die again; death no longer has dominion over Him. For the death He died He died to sin, once for all, but the life He lives He lives to God. So you also must consider yourselves dead to sin and *alive to God in Christ Jesus.* (Romans 6:8–11, emphasis added)

- And *because of Him you are in Christ Jesus*, who became to us wisdom from God, righteousness and sanctification and redemption, so that, as it is written, "Let the one who boasts, boast in the Lord." (1 Corinthians 1:30–31, emphasis added)

- *He is before all things, and in Him all things hold together.* And He is the head of the body, the church. He is the beginning, the firstborn from the dead, that in everything He might be preeminent. For in Him all the fullness of God was pleased to dwell, and through Him to reconcile to Himself all things, whether on earth or in heaven, making peace by the blood of His cross. (Colossians 1:17–20, emphasis added)

- And it is *God who establishes us with you in Christ*, and has anointed us, and who has also put His seal on us and given us His Spirit in our hearts as a guarantee. (2 Corinthians 1:21–22, emphasis added)

Paul's sentences well up with emotion and excitement. He passionately wants us to see what he has seen and to experience Christ's work. Hear the life in Paul's words as he explains the powerful work of God at work in those who are in Christ:

- In Him also you were circumcised with a circumcision made without hands, by putting off the body of the flesh, by the circumcision of Christ, having been *buried with Him in baptism*, in which you were also raised with Him through faith in the powerful working of God, who raised Him from the dead. And you, who were dead in your trespasses and the uncircumcision of your flesh, God made alive together with Him, having forgiven us all our trespasses, by canceling the record of debt that stood against us with its legal demands. This He set aside, nailing it to the cross. (Colossians 2:11–14, emphasis added)

- *In Him* we have redemption through His blood, the forgiveness of our trespasses, according to the riches of His grace, which He lavished upon us, in all wisdom and insight making known to us the mystery of His will, according to His purpose, which He set forth in Christ as a plan for the fullness of time, to unite all things in Him, things in heaven and things on earth.

  In Him we have obtained an inheritance, having been predestined according to the purpose of Him who works all things according to the counsel of His will, so that we who were the first to hope in Christ might be to the praise of His glory.

  In Him you also, when you heard the word of truth, the gospel of your salvation, and believed in Him, were sealed with the promised Holy Spirit, who is the guarantee of our inheritance until we acquire possession of it, to the praise of His glory. (Ephesians 1:7–14, emphasis added)

The branches have spoken! We abide, we dwell *in* Christ; we live *in* Christ; we have been baptized into His life. He is our rootstock, not susceptible to sin or death. Regardless of our life circumstances, we live in Christ; no matter where "here" is, we live in Christ; whether here on earth or in heaven, we live in Christ. The branches of The Vine, the apostles, wrote to call us to intimately know that we are "in Christ."

THE BRANCHES SPEAK: MY STORY

In 2005, the nurseries weren't able to provide us with year-old vines that had been grafted with Viognier, so we planted rootstock in the field and let it grow. The following year, we brought in a team of grafters. First they cut "bud wood" from an older Viognier field in our vineyard, and then they moved to the field where the rootstock was planted. I was driving my John Deere 5400 tractor, mowing weeds in the field adjacent to where the grafters settled in to work.

I parked my tractor and watched as the teams of two moved from one plant to the next. The lead person made a deep slice in the tender flesh of the rootstock, reached into his stash of Viognier wood, and made two precise cuts, separating the bud from the wood in the exact shape of the slice he had made in the rootstock. He placed the bud in the fresh cut and moved on to the next plant. His partner quickly tied the stretchy tape around the fresh wound and pushed soil around the base of the plant.

As I watched the plants being transformed by the hands of the grafters, my heart was touched by Jesus' words: "I am the vine; you are the branches." I thought, *He is my rootstock. I am that tiny little bud that has been placed into His life.* My mind raced through the words of the apostles: "*in* Christ." My breath was taken away when I thought of Peter's words: "By His wounds you have been healed." I wandered back to my tractor, fired it up, engaged the mower, and got back to work. As I went about my work, I gazed thoughtfully over the 300,000 grafted grapevines in my vineyard.

And I thanked God for speaking to me through the vine; I rejoiced in the work of God in me and at the thought of growing up in Him.

At the end of the day, I stood at the old sink in the laundry room where three generations before me had washed their hands after long days in the field. I glanced up at the old cupboard doors and thought of the Band-Aids that were always kept on the shelf inside. I pulled out a Band-Aid and turned it over and over in my fingers, meditating on the bleeding, healing wounds in my vineyard. I meditated on Jesus' words "I am the vine; you are the branches" and on His wounds for me. I thought of my wounds, some healed and some open. I prayed, "Lord, I need a Band-Aid on my heart." I placed the Band-Aid in my Bible to bookmark John 15 and went to the kitchen to prepare dinner for my family.

A few years later, I had the opportunity to visit a dear friend and mentor as he lay helpless in the hospital. He was weakened by the disease attacking his body. We visited for a while, and after a time, I shared that I had been praying for him and asked if I could pray with him. During the next visit, I did the same, and then I asked if I could tell him about my faith. Dennis was an exemplary leader, a rock in the industry and community. "In God we trust" was his motto, but I knew he didn't have a relationship with The Vine.

I didn't need to teach my mentor about grapevines or grafting, so I simply said, "You know how the bud is grafted into the rootstock. That is the picture of life in Christ. He is our rootstock, holy and not susceptible to disease or death. We are grafted into His life here and for eternity. It doesn't matter where here is; we live in Christ." Tears streamed down his face as the words touched his heart and soul with a vivid picture of life in Christ.

I walked into the hospital a few days later. His exhausted, tearful wife fell into my arms and said, "We've decided to shut off life support; he is ready to go home. Your words gave him courage to face death with the hope that he lives in Christ here just as he will in heaven." I stepped into his room in tears, and he said, "Cindy, at my memorial service, I want you to tell everyone what you told me about living in The Vine." A few days later, at home in the middle of his vineyard and surrounded by his family, he fell asleep in the arms of The Vine.

A few days after his death, I stood in front of my peers and tearfully told them what Dennis had asked me to say to them about his confident hope in Christ. I'll never know the fruit of that beautiful time of speaking to them what the vine had spoken to me. But I do know that my friend lived in The Vine while he was with us here and he lives in Christ today. We mourned his loss, and we rejoiced in the complete healing he enjoys and the life he lives in The Vine.

The grafted vines in my vineyard are a vivid reminder of my life in Christ. He is not susceptible to sin or death, and I live in His holy life. As I face challenges, joy, and pain, I do so in the context of living my life in Christ's holy life. He rose from the dead, and in Him, I rise to life from challenging circumstances. I live life fully and completely in relationship with The Vine. I live and grow in His life, both now and for eternity.

Earthly life is scary, and our balance is often rocked by circumstances beyond our control. The assurance we have in the Word of God is that we live in Christ. This fact has profound meaning in our fast-paced world. We can also be sure that Jesus' words and the words from the apostles have touched hearts and souls for generations and will be meaningful for all time.

THE BRANCHES SPEAK: YOUR STORY

Jesus' words, "I am the vine; you are the branches," are as alive today as the grapevines in my vineyard. By Christ's word and work, we have been grafted into His life through faith in Him. By His wounds, we have been healed. By His life flowing in us, we grow in Him. In Him, we are rooted and grounded, now and for eternity. Reflect on these questions in private, or discuss them in your small group:

1. What has The Vine spoken to you through this chapter?

2. Reflect on your "*in* Christ" life story. Share how God grafted you into His kingdom.

3. In Holy Baptism—or when we came to faith in Christ as adults—is the time at which we were grafted into Christ's life. What does it mean to you to "dwell" and to be "at home" in Christ?

4. Peter's words "by His wounds you have been healed" are past tense. What implications does that have for your life and faith?

Chapter Three

THE ROOTS OF THE VINE

THE VINE SPEAKS: MY FATHER'S VINEYARD

The intricate root system of the grapevine is made up of large roots that grow deep into the soil and smaller roots that grow closer to the surface. The large roots extend down into the harsh soils five, ten, even fifteen feet and spread horizontally as well. The vast majority of the root system is feeder roots that are found in the top eighteen inches of soil. Roots absorb water and nutrients that are used by the plant immediately. They also store carbohydrates and nutrients for future use.

The grafted vines that we purchase from the nurseries are one year old and have a well-established root system. We plant these new vines gently in the ground, root system loosely pointing down. The plants grow rapidly in our soil and produce some fruit in the first two years, but we cut away that fruit so the energy of the vine goes into growing and developing healthy roots. Roots of the grapevine continue to grow for the entire life of the plant and work year-round to give life to the plant.

Root System of Giant Oak Tree

Soil preparation before planting grapevines is critical to establishing and maintaining a healthy root system. Roots require adequate drainage and aeration. Before planting, the soil is dug up deeply, a process we call "ripping the soil." A large tractor pulls a five-foot-long, very thick steel implement called a "shank" that "rips" deeply in one direction. After the five-foot trench is dug, the five-foot shank is replaced by two three-foot

Ripper

shanks. The tractor pulls those shorter shanks diagonally across the original work.

Visualize the large tractor laboriously moving at one mile per hour to dig the soil five feet deep in one direction and three feet deep in another. We smooth out the bumpy soil by passing over it three times—with a cultivator, a disk, and a float drag. Irrigation lines are marked using precise GPS measurement, and mainline trenches are then dug and built. Organic compost is added to the soil as the final step before planting. All of this preparation takes place so the supple, tender roots have a home in which to grow and develop.

A healthy grapevine has a healthy root system. Conversely, we check unhealthy vines to assess the health of their root systems. Too much water, too little water, and not enough aeration are just a few of the problems we must identify and address to keep our vines healthy. For example, we once tore out an entire twenty-acre field that was only fifteen years old because when the vines were planted, the roots were forced into the harsh soils and pointed up, not down. The roots constricted over time, and the vines never thrived.

Healthy roots anchor the vines in the soil and provide stability and structure. The roots bear the weight of the trunks, vines, and branches and carry the weight of the fruit. They keep the vines grounded during storms and during the fruit-bearing season. Roots continue to grow down into the soil for the entire thirty- to fifty-year life of the vine.

THE VINE SPEAKS: JESUS' WORDS

I am the true vine, and My Father is the vinedresser. Every branch in Me that does not bear fruit He takes away, and every branch that does bear fruit He prunes, that it may bear more fruit. Already you are clean because of the word that I have spoken to you. Abide in Me, and I in you. As the branch cannot bear fruit by itself, unless it abides in the vine, neither can you, unless you abide in Me. I am the vine; you are the branches. Whoever abides in Me and I in

him, he it is that bears much fruit, for apart from Me you
can do nothing. (John 15:1–5)

Jesus, The Vine, is the rootstock into which we are grafted. By defini-
tion, for this chapter, I propose that The Vine is the root system up to the
graft union, which is located just above the soil. The root system of the
vine is unseen, but it works constantly to bring stability, water, and nutrients to the branches and the leaves.

John records this vision of Jesus speaking, declaring that He is the
root: "'I, Jesus, have sent My angel to testify to you about these things
for the churches. *I am the root* and the descendant of David, the bright
morning star.' The Spirit and the Bride say, 'Come.' And let the one who
hears say, 'Come.' And let the one who is thirsty come; let the one who
desires take the water of life without price" (Revelation 22:16–17, emphasis added).

Jesus, the root, is not susceptible to disease or death or sin. We are
grafted into His roots; therefore, we are not susceptible to disease or sin or
death. His roots provide stability for our lives; His roots provide refresh-
ment for our lives; His roots provide nutrients for our lives. We cannot
always see His work, but we are called to trust that He is always active.

The holy Root into which we have been grafted was formed before
the foundations of the world were created. Religious leaders of Jesus' day
could not see Him as God; they could not believe Him at His word or
embrace His work. They were infuriated during this conversation: "'Your
father Abraham rejoiced that he would see My day. He saw it and was glad.'
So the Jews said to Him, 'You are not yet fifty years old, and have You seen
Abraham?' Jesus said to them, 'Truly, truly, I say to you, before Abraham
was, I am'" (John 8:56–58).

Jesus prays this High Priestly Prayer to God just before His arrest, trial, and death. He tells us that our foundation, the root system into which we were grafted, existed before the foundation of the world. His work continues through time and eternity to bring about the will of God to keep us and sustain our lives in Him. Examine these verses in light of having been grafted into the rootstock, Jesus, The Vine:

> The glory that You have given Me I have given to them, that they may be one even as We are one, *I in them and You in Me,* that they may become perfectly one, so that the world may know that You sent Me and loved them even as You loved Me. Father, I desire that they also, whom You have given Me, may be with Me where I am, to see My glory that You have given Me because *You loved Me before the foundation of the world.* O righteous Father, even though the world does not know You, I know You, and these know that You have sent Me. I made known to them Your name, and I will continue to make it known, that *the love with which You have loved Me may be in them, and I in them.* (John 17:22–26, emphasis added)

Jesus, the root into which we are grafted, is our stability. Our Root and our Lifegiver was with God and was God before time began. Remember, also, that He dwells in us. Jesus, The Vine, our Rootstock, is with us always, even to the end of the age and for eternity. Ponder these well-known verses that Jesus spoke, in light of living life grafted into Him, our Rootstock:

- *Abide in Me, and I in you.* As the branch cannot bear fruit by itself, unless it *abides in the vine, neither can you, unless you abide in Me.* I am the vine; you are the branches. Whoever *abides in Me and I in him,* he it is that bears much fruit, for apart from Me you can do nothing. (John 15:4–5, emphasis added)

- Go therefore and make disciples of all nations, baptizing
them in the name of the Father and of the Son and of the
Holy Spirit, teaching them to observe all that I have commanded you. And behold, *I am with you always, to the end
of the age.*" (Matthew 28:19–20, emphasis added)

- "Behold, I am coming soon, bringing My recompense with
Me, to repay each one for what he has done. *I am the Alpha
and the Omega, the first and the last,* the beginning and the
end."

  Blessed are those who wash their robes, so that they may
  have the right to the tree of life and that they may enter the
  city by the gates. (Revelation 22:12–14, emphasis added)

The root system of the vine is always at work, even though we cannot see that work. Jesus, our rootstock, is always at work. He works God's
work—for us or in us or around us or through us—even though we cannot always see it. Jesus carried on this conversation with His disciples after
declaring Himself living water:

> Meanwhile the disciples were urging Him, saying, "Rab-
> bi, eat." But He said to them, "I have food to eat that you
> do not know about." So the disciples said to one another,
> "Has anyone brought Him something to eat?" Jesus said to
> them, *"My food is to do the will of Him who sent Me and to
> accomplish His work."* (John 4:31–34, emphasis added)

John's message is the message of life and growth through the work
and word of God. The roots of the vine work, even though we may not see
them at work. It can be easy to confuse our work as branches (receiving,
growing, and producing fruit) and the work of The Root. "Then [reli-
gious leaders] said to [Jesus], 'What must we do, to be doing the works of

God?' Jesus answered them, *'This is the work of God, that you believe in Him whom He has sent'"* (John 6:28–29, emphasis added).

These are profound words from The Vine to the hard-hearted, very confused, yet very religious people. His words drove these religious leaders to hate Him deeply. For others, these words caused them to say, "We're leaving You, Jesus, because these words are too hard." But others trusted the words of The Vine, and confessed, "Jesus, to whom shall we go? You have the words of eternal life."

We live in the holy root of The Vine. The Vine is always at work. We dwell in Him, and His energy nourishes us; His living water gives us stability. The very alive relationship we have in The Vine doesn't end there! Jesus dwells in us. We are called to grow and bear fruit from the context of a relationship that is rooted and grounded *in* The Vine and the life of The Vine in us.

THE BRANCHES SPEAK: THE APOSTLES' WORDS

Paul's language is alive with language of having been grafted into the vine. Paul speaks to a culture that was asking "Who is saved—Jews or Gentiles or both?" and "Whom did Jesus come to save?" Our fast-paced culture asks, "Who am I, and where in this vast world do I dwell?" Paul comforts our hearts with these "grafted into Christ" words:

> *If the root is holy, so are the branches.* But if some of the branches were broken off, and you, although a wild olive shoot, were grafted in among the others and now share in the nourishing root of the olive tree, do not be arrogant toward the branches. If you are, remember *it is not you who support the root, but the root that supports you.* (Romans 11:16–18, emphasis added)

Paul used an olive tree as his example, but the same practices are applied to grapevines. His prayers and words of encouragement reflect the language of being rooted in Christ:

- For this reason I bow my knees before the Father, from whom every family in heaven and on earth is named, that according to the riches of His glory He may grant you to be strengthened with power through His Spirit in your inner being, so that Christ may dwell in your hearts through faith—that you, *being rooted and grounded in love,* may have strength to comprehend with all the saints what is the breadth and length and height and depth, and to know the love of Christ that surpasses knowledge, that you may be filled with all the fullness of God. (Ephesians 3:14–19, emphasis added)

- Therefore, as you received Christ Jesus the Lord, so *walk in Him, rooted and built up in Him and established in the faith,* just as you were taught, abounding in thanksgiving. (Colossians 2:6–7, emphasis added)

In our vineyard, we can see what is taking place in the vine above the ground. We know that far more has been established in the working of the plant in the root system below ground. We know by what is happening above that an equal amount of energy is moving and producing below. Even if we dug up the established roots, we would not be able to see what is taking place inside the roots.

Paul pondered the question of being established in Christ as he preached the love of God in Christ to new Christians. My family heritage in Paso Robles was established in 1884. Christ, our rootstock, was established before the foundations of the world, and in Him we are rooted and grounded. Many seek to be established, rooted, and grounded by deeds of righteousness. But Scripture tells us that we are grafted into Christ through His word and work alone. The holiness of our life is by Christ's righteousness, the holy root. Paul says:

> For I bear them witness that they have a zeal for God, but not according to knowledge. For, being ignorant of the righteousness of God, and seeking to establish their own, they did not submit to God's righteousness. For Christ is the end of the law for righteousness to everyone who believes. (Romans 10:2–4)

Paul's language comes alive within the context of God's work of grafting us into Christ's life. We live, we dwell, and we abide in Christ. Reflect on these beautiful words from Paul's letters as he reflects "in Christ" language.

- If in Christ we have hope in this life only, we are of all people most to be pitied. But in fact Christ has been raised from the dead, the firstfruits of those who have fallen asleep. For as by a man came death, by a man has come also the resurrection of the dead. For as in Adam all die, so also in Christ shall all be made alive. (1 Corinthians 15:19–22)

- Therefore, if anyone is in Christ, he is a new creation. The old has passed away; behold, the new has come. All this is from God, who through Christ reconciled us to Himself and gave us the ministry of reconciliation; that is, in Christ God was reconciling the world to Himself, not counting their trespasses against them, and entrusting to us the message of reconciliation. Therefore, we are ambassadors for Christ, God making His appeal through us. We implore you on behalf of Christ, be reconciled to God. For our sake He made Him to be sin who knew no sin, so that in Him we might become the righteousness of God. (2 Corinthians 5:17–21)

- Now if we have died with Christ, we believe that we will also live with Him. We know that Christ, being raised from the dead, will never die again; death no longer has dominion over Him. For the death He died He died to sin, once for all, but the life He lives He lives to God. So you also must consider yourselves dead to sin and alive to God in Christ Jesus. (Romans 6:8–11)

- Blessed be the God and Father of our Lord Jesus Christ, who has blessed us in Christ with every spiritual blessing in the heavenly places, even as He chose us in Him before the foundation of the world, that we should be holy and blameless before Him. (Ephesians 1:3–4)

Living vines need oxygen both aboveground and below to thrive. Ponder these parallels: God tills the soil. God breathes His breath of life into our lives. His breath is the oxygen in the soil of our lives that we need to receive, grow, thrive, and bear fruit. Paul spoke of the breath of life in whom we live and move and have our being:

The God who made the world and everything in it, being Lord of heaven and earth, does not live in temples made by man, nor is He served by human hands, as though He needed anything, since He Himself gives to all mankind life and breath and everything. And He made from one man every nation of mankind to live on all the face of the earth, having determined allotted periods and the boundaries of their dwelling place, that they should seek God, and perhaps feel their way toward Him and find Him. Yet He is actually not far from each one of us, for "'In Him we live and move and have our being' as even some of your

own poets have said, 'For we are indeed His offspring.'"
(Acts 17:24–28)

We studied Peter's declaration that we have been "healed by Christ's wounds" in chapter 2 as we discussed grafting. Peter's words take on greater richness for our study as we look at these verses again, this time from the perspective of the root system bearing the weight of the plant and giving it stability. Peter declares:

> He Himself bore our sins in His body on the tree, that we might die to sin and live to righteousness. By His wounds you have been healed. For you were straying like sheep, but have now returned to the Shepherd and Overseer of your souls. (1 Peter 2:24–25)

Peter's words take on greater richness as we consider that they are a quote from Isaiah, with a beautiful twist. Please take time to ponder Isaiah's words foretelling Jesus' work, and compare Isaiah's words with Peter's words:

> Who has believed what he has heard from us? And to whom has the arm of the LORD been revealed? For He grew up before Him like a young plant, and like a root out of dry ground; He had no form or majesty that we should look at Him, and no beauty that we should desire Him. He was despised and rejected by men; a man of sorrows, and acquainted with grief; and as one from whom men hide their faces He was despised, and we esteemed Him not.
>
> Surely He has borne our griefs and carried our sorrows; yet we esteemed Him stricken, smitten by God, and afflicted. But He was pierced for our transgressions; He was crushed for our iniquities; upon Him was the chastisement

that brought us peace, and with His wounds we are healed. All we like sheep have gone astray; we have turned—every one—to His own way; and the LORD has laid on Him the iniquity of us all. (Isaiah 53:1–6)

Isaiah and Peter declared that the weight of our sins was placed on Jesus, who had lived a perfect life and turned His face toward the cross in obedience to God's demand for a perfect sacrifice. Isaiah and Peter call us to believe that Jesus, the holy root, bore the weight of our sin. Isaiah and Peter call us to trust that we don't bear the weight or responsibility of restoring the relationship between God and us. We are free from the task of bearing the weight of our sin.

The sheep have gone astray in Isaiah's words; the sheep have returned in Peter's words. This is the truth of life in The Vine: God fulfills His promises. We are grafted into the life of The Vine and His holy roots; by His wounds we have been healed. As we grow up in Him, we continue to learn to trust that this action has taken place for us.

THE BRANCHES SPEAK: MY STORY

My grandmother grew up in the home in which I now live. Her parents purchased this land and built the house in 1921. She and Grandpa lived here until 1972, when they sold the land to my parents. I adored my grandmother. I admired her love for learning and her ability and desire for profound conversation. She was my go-to gal.

Just days after her 97th birthday, she coughed and struggled to speak under the weight of the pneumonia that stuck in her chest. I said, "Grandma, you don't have to talk." She replied, "Then you talk." I told her that Jesus' words "I am the Good Shepherd" were the theme of my next

Bible study. I told her about my discoveries in the Gospel of John and the fun I was having listening to the vineyard and the vines speak.

Grandma said, "Cindy, you are so faithful." I placed my head on her arm and cried, knowing that she didn't have many more days on this earth to be my mentor and friend. I looked up, stroked her face, and said, "Grandma, Jesus is faithful." After a few quiet moments passed, she replied, "Cindy, that's what brings you around." Time stood still as her words sunk deep into my soul.

A week later, I walked into her room, and I kissed and hugged her. I sat at her side and stroked her. Within moments, she took a deep breath, a final breath. The Vine, the life in whom she had been rooted and grounded, held her just as closely after she took her last breath as He had while she was breathing and her heart was beating. She was rooted and grounded in The Vine for eternity. She lived in Christ during her earthly life, and she lives in Him in her death.

Grandma's whole life was a witness to God's work to "bring her around." She grew up in Him and she died in Him. An oak tree is planted in her memory on top of a hill, which is now named "G——ma's Hill." As

Four Generations

I look out over the vineyard from Grandma's tree, I am reminded of her words and her faith in Christ. I reflect on being proud of my roots and my heritage. I'm also proud that she trusted that in Christ, we have a holy, healthy heritage and a hopeful future.

My heritage is healthy and strong, like our vineyards. Upon closer examination, however, some of my heritage is not so healthy. I am honored to live in an established vineyard on property our family established in 1920 in a community our family helped establish in 1884. My seven-generation heritage makes me proud, and I display that heritage and tell my story in my museum-like tasting room. Upon first glance, everything looks perfect, with no bumps in the road, no challenges or pain. But as beautiful as my heritage is, there *are* bumps, challenges, and pain.

Examining my roots has been an important part of my growing in The Vine. Judging previous generations would be easy, but not fruitful. My purpose in taking a deeper look at my heritage is growth. I acknowledge that my family members did the best they could with what they learned from their family members. That, however, doesn't stop my longing for growth and health and change. Taking a deep look is hard, but it is good, and it is the way of growth. These examples from my life may resonate with your experiences. If not, please take time to examine your heritage from a healthy desire to grow.

One unhealthy aspect of my family roots is the long-standing desire to make everything look perfect on the outside. Churches are filled with people who genuinely love Jesus and know their need for forgiveness and mercy. They receive Christ's mercy and forgiveness, and then they depart in peace to return to the very same life. Everything looks perfect on the outside. But underneath are breaking hearts and aching souls that long for peace and comfort. Many people are not interested in growing or living; they are just resigned to live the motto "this is the way it is."

"This is the way it is" is much easier than saying, "I'm not satisfied with the way things have always been; I want to grow." But not growing, not even desiring growth, is contrary to God's Word and God's clear desire for us. It would be foolish to think that an infant or child can take care of his own physical needs. It is foolish to think that an infant, child, teenager, or young adult can grow up on her own spiritually, emotionally, or in matters of the heart. It is foolish to think that we have fully matured and that we don't need to continue growing. But we don't know how to cry out and say "I cannot do this myself."

Another unhealthy aspect of my roots is that open discussion about emotional pain or struggle was not welcome. Painful events were not discussed so that children could learn from them. Some family members struggled silently, longing for more honesty, authenticity, and openness. Others were resigned to the status quo. Still others know that there is more, but they don't care. For some, caring is too hard, so they quit caring.

As I struggled through the challenges of an unhealthy marriage, all of this unhealthy heritage and more rose to the surface. My home life was volatile while my church life looked perfect. I thought I was the first in my family to get a divorce. I wasn't. I lived in silence for years, believing I needed to "just deal with it; this is the life I chose."

Living in The Vine means we are grafted into His holy roots. In Christ, we have a healthy, holy heritage. We examine our earthly heritage so we see how to grow more fully into our holy heritage in Christ. We live *in* this world, but we are not *of* this world because we are grafted into Christ's life and live in His holy roots.

The Root calls us to live life in His life; the Root calls us to grow up in the knowledge of His stability and the nutrients He provides. The Root calls us to grow up in our understanding of His mercy and to grow in love and mercy toward self and others. Growing is the only option in the vineyard; growing is the only option in our flesh-on-flesh, grafted-in relationship with Christ.

THE BRANCHES SPEAK: YOUR STORY

Reflect on these questions in private, or discuss them with your small group. Share only as much as you feel comfortable sharing. Share more with God in prayer.

1. What has The Vine spoken to you through this chapter?
2. What does being rooted and grounded in Christ mean for your life today?
3. What verses mean the most to you as you reflect on Christ, our rootstock, and on life in His holy life?
4. What wisdom can you share from your roots, your heritage, about being rooted and grounded in Christ? What challenges do you face as you reflect on unhealthy aspects of your earthly roots?
5. How does reflecting on living "in Christ, rooted in Him" change your perspective?

Chapter Four

THE ENERGY OF THE VINE

THE VINE SPEAKS: MY FATHER'S VINEYARD

S ap is a clear, flavorless substance that flows from the roots throughout every cell of the vine. It flows year-round inside the grapevine, carrying nutrients and water to the entire vine. It provides the vine and the branches with the energy needed for them to grow and produce fruit. Sap is the lifeblood of the vine.

The energy in the sap flow changes during different growing seasons. The sap flows slowly from December to March, as the dormant vines store up energy for the coming growing season. From April to July, the sap flows quickly as its energy is directed toward growing shoots and leaf surface. The energy of the plant shifts again from August through October in order to produce sugar in the clusters of fruit, but the sap continues to flow quickly. After harvest, the sap flow slows until the vines go completely dormant after the first heavy frosts.

When the vine is wounded by pruning shears or the grafter's knife, it bleeds sap. The healing property of the grapevine goes to work, making a scab as soon as a wound is made. The wound heals quickly, and the scab

Sap Flowing out of Wound

grows new cells to cover the wound. The healed wound becomes a woody scar on the plant, which remains for the life of the plant.

A trained eye, at just the right time in the spring, can see the lifeblood of the vine. As the soil and air warm and sap flow quickens, sap can be seen dripping from unhealed wounds. I've seen this energy, this sap dripping off the plant, as the late afternoon sun glistens off the droplets. The energy of the plant pushes so rapidly that the sap drips out of the wounds in the vine rather than staying in the plant. The sap can be seen until a scab hardens over the wound. Within a few days, a scab has formed, and the sap is again contained within the plant.

Sap flow, for the most part, cannot be seen, but we trust that it takes place year-round. Shoots, leaves, and fruit begin to wilt immediately after they are taken off the plant because they are cut off from the sap flow. The sap is the life, the energy, the blood of the vine. Sap flow is essential to the life of the vine.

THE VINEDRESSER SPEAKS:
GOD'S WORD FROM THE OLD TESTAMENT

Grapevines have been studied for centuries, as have animal and human life. Scientists haven't even scratched the surface of the complexity of the vine or created life. The heart and blood vessels, the lungs, the liver and kidneys, the bladder, the stomach, and the intestines are a profound picture of nourishment and cleansing. God's creation is astounding, and the intricacies of the grapevine are part of His masterful work.

God spoke and created life. By His design, every living creature and plant has blood or sap within. Blood or sap distributes nutrients and water. The energy of that lifeblood flows while the creature or plant is alive. It stops flowing when the creature or plant dies or is cut off from the life source. Every aspect of life relates back to the lifeblood and cleansing within.

God set apart the children of Israel so they would be a light to draw others to His life. The laws God commanded certainly set them apart. As we fast-forward to today, we can comprehend these Old Testament laws in light of the lifeblood of the vine. God's laws help sustain life and help us see the fulfillment of all law in the lifeblood of Christ, given for us. Our atonement came through the lifeblood of the Lamb.

In the Old Testament, the people of God were commanded not to drink or eat the blood of animals. Grafted into Christ's life, we, the people of God, are invited to eat His flesh and drink His blood for forgiveness and eternal life. Keeping in mind our study of the sap flow of the vine, review these Old Testament commands regarding the cleansing of lepers and atonement:

- For the life of the flesh is in the blood, and I have given it for you on the altar to make atonement for your souls, for it is the blood that makes atonement by the life. Therefore I have said to the people of Israel, No person among you shall eat blood, neither shall any stranger who sojourns among you eat blood.

  Any one also of the people of Israel, or of the strangers who sojourn among them, who takes in hunting any beast or bird that may be eaten shall pour out its blood and cover it with earth. For the life of every creature is its blood: its blood is its life. Therefore I have said to the people of Israel, you shall not eat the blood of any creature, for the life of every creature is its blood. Whoever eats it shall be cut off. (Leviticus 17:11–14)

- Only be sure that you do not eat the blood, for the blood is the life, and you shall not eat the life with the flesh. You shall not eat it; you shall pour it out on the earth like water. You shall not eat it, that all may go well with you and with your children after you, when you do what is right in the sight of the LORD. (Deuteronomy 12:23–25)

The words of God in His commands for the children of Israel were given that they would live and multiply and dwell in the land (see Deuteronomy 8). True life, however, came only in and through the hope of the promise, and in and through the lifeblood of Jesus, The Vine. Jesus fulfilled all of the commands and promises of God. He brought true life and light in His perfect life, His suffering, His death, His resurrection, and His ascension. The Vine brought life by spilling His lifeblood, His energy, for us.

In the Old Testament, the people of God were commanded not to eat the blood because in it was the life of the animal. In the New Testament, Jesus, the perfect Lamb of God, commands us to eat His flesh and drink His blood, for in His life is our life. His lifeblood is forgiveness, life, and salvation. The children of Israel were set apart because they didn't eat certain meats or consume the blood. Christians are set apart because, by Jesus' command, they eat and drink His flesh and blood for life.

THE VINE SPEAKS: JESUS' WORDS

I am the true vine, and My Father is the vinedresser. Every branch in Me that does not bear fruit He takes away, and every branch that does bear fruit He prunes, that it may bear more fruit. Already you are clean because of the word that I have spoken to you. Abide in Me, and I in you. As the branch cannot bear fruit by itself, unless it abides in the vine, neither can you, unless you abide in Me. I am the vine; you are the branches. Whoever abides in Me and I in him, he it is that bears much fruit, for apart from Me you can do nothing. (John 15:1–5)

Jesus said, "I am the vine, you are the branches. Apart from Me you can do nothing." His words come alive with meaning as we meditate on the sap flow, the lifeblood of the vine. A branch or leaf or fruit cut off of the vine withers immediately. Sap flow, like the blood flow in our human body, is absolutely necessary to life. The energy of the sap flow through the grapevine is always working to deliver nutrients and water. In a similar way, the energy of The Vine is always working to deliver nutrients, to cleanse and deposit oxygen to every cell of our bodies.

Christ's energy flows through the graft union, through His wounds, into our life. His holy life breeds life in us and through us. His energy breeds energy. The energy of belief and faith, growth and change wells up within us as we receive the life He came to give, as we feed on His lifeblood to receive the nourishment of our souls.

Jesus still works as His Word goes forth in us and through us. His work and words—"Come forth"; "Your faith has made you well"; "Rise up"—are living words, filled with energy for you and for me. The Vine speaks, "Grow up in Me." His work and word, "This is My body"; "this is My blood," for forgiveness and eternal life are His life energy for you and for me. Healing may not take the form we pray for or choose right here right now, but we are alive, grafted into His life. Our aliveness is eternally in The Vine.

Jesus' words of life created energy in the lives of His followers. Jesus' words also met with tremendous negative energy. The energy of religious leaders welled up within them, against Him, as they raged at words they thought were an affront to Old Testament law. They could not see. They were blind to His words and to the Word of life:

So Jesus said to them, "Truly, truly, I say to you, unless you eat the flesh of the Son of Man and drink His blood, you have no life in you. Whoever feeds on My flesh and drinks My blood has eternal life, and I will raise him up on the last day. For My flesh is true food, and My blood is true drink. Whoever feeds on My flesh and drinks My blood abides in Me, and I in him. As the living Father sent Me, and I live because of the Father, so whoever feeds on Me, he also will live because of Me." (John 6:53–57)

They could not see Jesus' life as the fulfillment of God's commands, the God of the old covenant. Jesus created tremendous controversy with His words to the religious leaders. Their negative energy, their angry hearts and minds, hung Him on the cross. Nevertheless, Jesus' work was an extension of His Father's work. Jesus spent His energy watching God work and doing God's work. John records:

Jesus answered them, "My Father is working until now, and I am working." This was why the Jews were seeking all the more to kill Him, because not only was He breaking the Sabbath, but He was even calling God His own Father, making Himself equal with God. So Jesus said to them, "Truly, truly, I say to you, the Son can do nothing of His own accord, but only what He sees the Father doing. For whatever the Father does, that the Son does likewise. For the Father loves the Son and shows Him all that He Himself is doing. And greater works than these will He show Him, so that you may marvel. For as the Father raises the dead and gives them life, so also the Son gives life to whom He will." (John 5:17–21, emphasis added)

Jesus worked the work of restoration, the work of creation of faith, the work of healing, of mercy, of raising the dead, and of being life and love. Jesus' work fulfilled Isaiah's words. Think of Jesus' energy, the giving of His life energy, in these words: "The Spirit of the Lord is upon Me, because He has anointed Me to proclaim good news to the poor. He has sent Me to proclaim liberty to the captives and recovering of sight to the blind, to set at liberty those who are oppressed, to proclaim the year of the Lord's favor" (Luke 4:18–19; see Isaiah 61).

John's Gospel takes on profound richness in light of the sap flow, the energy of The Vine. John's words are energy-filled words poured out on the pages of his Gospel so we might believe deeply that Jesus' word and work give life. John believed that Jesus' life was his lifeblood and that through His words, Jesus' energy is poured out for us and in us and through us. Meditate on these words from John's heart. As you do, notice also the negative energy emanating from the religious leaders:

- In the beginning was the Word, and the Word was with God, and the Word was God. He was in the beginning with God. All things were made through Him, and without Him was not any thing made that was made. In Him was life, and the life was the light of men. The light shines in the darkness, and the darkness has not overcome it. (John 1:1–5)

- In the temple He found those who were selling oxen and sheep and pigeons, and the money-changers sitting there. And making a whip of cords, He drove them all out of the temple, with the sheep and oxen. And He poured out the coins of the money-changers and overturned their tables. And He told those who sold the pigeons, "Take these things away; do not make My Father's house a house of trade." His disciples remembered that it was written, "Zeal for Your house will consume Me." (John 2:14–17)

- For God so loved the world, that He gave His only Son, that whoever believes in Him should not perish but have eternal life. For God did not send His Son into the world to condemn the world, but in order that the world might be saved through Him. (John 3:16–17)

- Jesus answered her, "If you knew the gift of God, and who it is that is saying to you, 'Give Me a drink,' you would have asked Him, and He would have given you living water." The woman said to Him, "Sir, You have nothing to draw water with, and the well is deep. Where do You get that living water? Are You greater than our father Jacob? He gave us the well and drank from it himself, as did his sons and his livestock." Jesus said to her, "Everyone who drinks of this water will be thirsty again, but whoever drinks of the water that I will give him will never be thirsty again. The water that I will give him will become in him a spring of water welling up to eternal life." (John 4:10–14)

- Jesus said to her, "Woman, believe Me, the hour is coming when neither on this mountain nor in Jerusalem will you worship the Father. You worship what you do not know; we worship what we know, for salvation is from the Jews. But the hour is coming, and is now here, when the true worshipers will worship the Father in spirit and truth, for the Father is seeking such people to worship Him. God is spirit, and those who worship Him must worship in spirit and truth." The woman said to Him, "I know that Messiah is coming (He who is called Christ). When He comes, He will tell us all things." Jesus said to her, "I who speak to you am He." (John 4:21–26)

- Truly, truly, I say to you, an hour is coming, and is now here, when the dead will hear the voice of the Son of God, and those who hear will live. For as the Father has life in Himself, so He has granted the Son also to have life in Himself. (John 5:25–26)

- You search the Scriptures because you think that in them you have eternal life; and it is they that bear witness about Me, yet you refuse to come to Me that you may have life. I do not receive glory from people. But I know that you do not have the love of God within you. I have come in My Father's name, and you do not receive Me. If another comes in his own name, you will receive him. How can you believe, when you receive glory from one another and do not seek the glory that comes from the only God? Do not think that I will accuse you to the Father. There is one who accuses you: Moses, on whom you have set your hope. For if you believed Moses, you would believe Me; for he wrote of Me. But if you do not believe his writings, how will you believe My words? (John 5:39–47)

- It is the Spirit who gives life; the flesh is no help at all. The words that I have spoken to you are spirit and life. (John 6:63)

Jesus' word and work are life; Jesus' word and work are life for us and nurture life *in* us; Jesus' word and work nurture life *through* us. His lifeblood cleanses us and frees us to live life full of energy in Him. We have been grafted into His life, and the sap flows through The Vine into the branches, and we bear fruit.

THE BRANCHES SPEAK: THE APOSTLES' WORDS

The apostles heard and saw Jesus' energy flow through His word and work. They saw Christ's lifeblood spill out, and they saw the Spirit being poured out on them on Pentecost. Having witnessed Christ's life and energy at work, they, as branches in The Vine, spoke life. They can't contain the energy within them because it was Christ at work breeding life through His life.

Paul witnessed Christ's energy and life when He called him from a life of spending his energy plotting and murdering to one of healing. Paul called the people of Colossae to a rich understanding of Christ at work in him and in them. Those same words call us to contemplate the energy of God, the power of God at work in us, bringing life, growth, and eternal life. Paul calls us to grasp the truth of our lives grafted into Christ and His life dwelling in us:

> To them God chose to make known how great among the Gentiles are the riches of the glory of this mystery, which is Christ in you, the hope of glory. Him we proclaim, warning everyone and teaching everyone with all wisdom, that we may present everyone mature in Christ. For this I toil, struggling with all His energy that He powerfully works within me. (Colossians 1:27–29)

The energy of the sap flow in the vine is incredible, and how much more so is the energy flow through The Vine to us! We are rooted and grounded in love, rooted and grounded in Christ. Christ dwells in us; we dwell in Christ. His energy and life work continuously—calling, healing, restoring—in us and through us. Paul's words come to life for us; his prayer becomes our prayer as we reflect on God in Christ at work in these words:

> For this reason, because I have heard of your faith in the Lord Jesus and your love toward all the saints, I do not cease to give thanks for you, remembering you in my prayers,

that the God of our Lord Jesus Christ, the Father of glory, may give you the Spirit of wisdom and of revelation in the knowledge of Him, having the eyes of your hearts enlightened, that you may know what is the hope to which He has called you, what are the riches of His glorious inheritance in the saints, and what is the immeasurable greatness of His power toward us who believe, according to the working of His great might that He worked in Christ when He raised Him from the dead and seated Him at His right hand in the heavenly places, far above all rule and authority and power and dominion, and above every name that is named, not only in this age but also in the one to come. And He put all things under His feet and gave Him as head over all things to the church, which is His body, the fullness of Him who fills all in all. (Ephesians 1:15–23)

Paul's words to the people in Ephesus build into a magnificent crescendo as he reflects on and proclaims the energy of God. With these same words, he calls us to comprehend the work of God: the same energy at work when God raised Jesus from the dead is at work in us in this moment. The Greek word Paul chose to describe Christ's power or energy is the word from which we derive the word *dynamite*. Consider Paul's powerful words as we meditate on Christ's energy at work:

- For through the law I died to the law, so that I might live to God. I have been crucified with Christ. It is no longer I who live, but Christ who lives in me. And the life I now live in the flesh I live by faith in the Son of God, who loved me and gave Himself for me. I do not nullify the grace of God, for if righteousness were through the law, then Christ died for no purpose. (Galatians 2:19–21)

- For this reason I bow my knees before the Father, from

whom every family in heaven and on earth is named, that according to the riches of His glory He may grant you to be strengthened with power through His Spirit in your inner being, so that Christ may dwell in your hearts through faith—that you, being rooted and grounded in love, may have strength to comprehend with all the saints what is the breadth and length and height and depth, and to know the love of Christ that surpasses knowledge, that you may be filled with all the fullness of God. (Ephesians 3:14–19)

Christ's lifeblood, His energy, is at work in us and gives us hope. His energy brings focus and clarity when we have energy and even when we don't. We live our lives alive, grafted into the life of The Vine.

John's words also come alive with life and meaning as we reflect on the energy at work in his use of the words *life* and *light*. John began his Gospel proclaiming Jesus as life and light in contrast to the darkness that did not comprehend the light. John records Jesus' words, "I am the vine, you are the branches. Apart from Me you can do nothing," just before Jesus spilled His lifeblood on the darkness of the cross for the life of the world.

Jesus' energy, His life, achieved healing and accomplished the perfection God demands. The cross was where His life, His energy, was spilled for the life of the world in order to accomplish His word and work. The empty tomb calls us to trust that "He Himself bore our sins in His body on the tree, that we might die to sin and live to righteousness. By His wounds you have been healed" (1 Peter 2:24). We have been grafted into The Vine; we dwell in the flesh, in the lifeblood of The Vine; He dwells in us. We died with Him, are healed by His blood, and have risen with Him.

John begs us to "get it," to grasp hold of the promise of Jesus' life in us and our life in Him. He says, "There is so much more I could tell you about the word of life." At the end of his Gospel, John records, "Now Jesus did many other signs in the presence of the disciples, which are not written in this book; but these are written so that you may believe that Jesus is the Christ, the Son of God, and that by believing you may have life in His name" (John 20:30–31).

The Branches Speak: My Story

My friend and I walked the dusty roads of Steinbeck Vineyards, getting to know each other better. She was fascinated by the grapevines, and I welcomed the opportunity to talk about my family vineyards. We traded life stories as we walked and talked. She commented that my steps were unsteady and my eyes were always glued on the path ahead. I said, "I've had a lot of injuries and accidents, and I'm just being careful not to stumble." She said, "You need to trust."

I was a very active child, full of life and energy. With today's wisdom-filled hindsight, I understand that my eyes were always on a goal and my heart always set on getting to it quickly, so I paid little attention to what was between me and my goal. That tendency, coupled with a six-hundred-acre playground, farm life, and motorized vehicles led to many trips to the hospital for stitches and x-rays and admissions. Pain and healing were part of my everyday life.

I said to my friend, "Trust? I don't know how to do that." My friend said, "I'll go with you to every place on this ranch where you've gotten hurt. We'll talk about the specific injury and ask God to help you learn to be careful, to learn to trust."

Then she thought about how long it would take us (there were a lot of places) and said, "I changed my mind. Let's lie down here and give these injuries and your wounds to God." The rain fell on us as we lay in the wet grass and mud in the middle of Row 124. We talked about so many injuries, so much healing left to do, so much pain. We talked about God's desire for life and healing and wholeness. We prayed for strength and courage to face what hadn't been working and to turn toward a greater trust in God's work for us and in us.

Row 124 became the row for leaving "stuff" behind. For some time now, we have journeyed to Row 124. We choose a rock along the way, verbalize whatever "it" is, and place the rock in Row 124 with a prayer that God take it because we don't want it. The energy I spent carrying my stuff has been shifted to giving it to God and praying for trust. When I lose

Leaving It in Row 124

sight of the fact that I have given it to God, my friend says, "If you want it back, let's walk out to Row 124, pick up that rock, and bring in right back here with us." Point taken.

The pile of rocks in Row 124 has grown because others have journeyed there with me and given their own "it" to God. The rocks are a vivid representation of our burdens, our pain, and the stuff we unnecessarily carry. They belong to Row 124, the soil, and to God. The pile will continue to grow because God can handle it and we don't need it. As I have learned to take care of my soul and spirit, I am learning to care for my body as well.

Months later, during our weekly walk, my friend and I were contemplating the energy God worked through leaving a rock in the field. She said, "Let's run!" I exclaimed, "Run?! I'm barely getting used to walking without getting injured." She grabbed my hand, and off we sprinted across the uneven soil, surrounded by growth and the life of the vines. The quarter-mile row seemed short, and when we paused at the end of it to catch our breath, we looked at the number at the end of the row—55.

Row 55 has become a rejoicing row, a row for letting go and trusting. There is no pile of rocks here, only a few grains of sand and some beautiful stones scattered to represent freedom in Christ. We kneel at Row 55 to rejoice in growth and healing, to celebrate courage and eyes wide open to God's word and work, to honor God's work in us and through us. Row 55 is not a leaving place; it is a growing and celebrating place. You're welcome to journey to Paso Robles and place your burden in Row 124 and rejoice in Row 55.

The vines have loudly spoken of another aspect of healing. I was walking by myself one day and was astounded by a breathtaking sight: sap was dripping from every wound on a newly pruned vineyard. Those wounds spoke to me of Christ's life flowing in me and through me. I am grafted into His life, rooted and grounded in Him; He dwells in my heart. An energy shift took place in me that day.

I thought about the exorbitant amount of energy I spent trying to carry on my own a marriage that was not healthy or fruitful. I was forced to admit the pain my marriage caused me. And admitting that led me to further honesty—I didn't want to be alive. Acknowledging my pain took tremendous energy and courage. But seeing the sap flow from the wounded vines gave me deep hope of Christ's life in me. The Vine's words and the imagery in this photo kept me alive during the challenges I faced.

When I meditate on the energy the body puts toward healing a wound, I am reminded to trust more deeply in Christ's energy at work in me, for me. His lifeblood heals, cleanses, and breeds life. The sap flows in the vine at all times. Christ's energy flows in us at all times, to every cell of

our being. We trust His word and work as it brings healing, energy, and life into our lives.

THE BRANCHES SPEAK: YOUR STORY

Discuss the following questions with your small group. Share only as much as you feel comfortable sharing. Share more with God in prayer.

1. What has The Vine spoken to you through this chapter on energy flow?
2. What areas of your life could use an energy shift?
3. What would you write on a rock to leave in Row 124?
4. What meaningful ways have you learned to "cast all your cares on Him"?
5. Visualize your Row 55. List ways to celebrate Christ's energy and nurturing life in you.

Chapter Five

The Vinedresser

The Vine Speaks: My Father's Vineyard

Grapevines need a lot of care in order to live and grow and bear fruit. That caretaker is formally called a *viticulturist,* informally called a "grape grower" or a "wine grower." The grape grower oversees the vineyard, identifies work that needs to be done, gives instructions to workers, and oversees their work. Training, either at a formal or informal level, is necessary to be a good viticulturist. Years of experience add practical application and wisdom to the grape grower's résumé.

Our viticulturist, our grape grower, gardener, and manager, is my father. His word is final. He takes every necessary step to grow quality fruit. My father prepares the soil so that newly planted vines thrive. My father orders vines from the nursery to his specifications. He inspects the plants when they are delivered and watches over the planting process. My father cares for each plant individually and the vineyard as a whole. As the vines mature, he tends to every aspect of their well-being.

My Father

My father is faithful and vigilant as he protects and cares for the vines in our vineyard. The casual eye sees the beauty in the vineyard, and Dad does too, but he is also looking for problems to solve and work to be done. When problems are beyond his knowledge and ability, he hires experts to assess and give recommendations so our vines can be brought back to health and balance. My father, if necessary, works 24–7 during the busiest seasons of the year.

Our grapevines have no choice but to submit to the care of the viticulturist. They don't know what they need, but the caring grape grower does. Without proper care, grapevines would grow into an unkempt, unruly, overgrown mess, and the quality of the fruit would be diminished. Wineries would not purchase our grapes, and we wouldn't want to place our name on a bottle of wine made with poor fruit.

The eyes and hands of the grape grower are consistent with these goals: growth, life, health, and fruit production. Dad regularly walks or rides a quad through the vineyards to make sure our goals are met. He looks carefully at the leaves and digs up the soil. He watches the weather forecast and takes measures to care for the vines accordingly. Dad has complete oversight. He is passionate, persistent, and patient as he works. He is a great example of an expert, loving vinedresser. His example launches us into Jesus' words, "I am the true vine. My father is the vinedresser."

THE VINE SPEAKS: JESUS' WORDS

I am the true vine, and My Father is the vinedresser. Every branch in Me that does not bear fruit He takes away, and every branch that does bear fruit He prunes, that it may bear more fruit. Already you are clean because of the word that I have spoken to you. Abide in Me, and I in you. As

89

the branch cannot bear fruit by itself, unless it abides in the vine, neither can you, unless you abide in Me. I am the vine; you are the branches. Whoever abides in Me and I in him, he it is that bears much fruit, for apart from Me you can do nothing. (John 15:1–5)

Jesus calls His Father The Vinedresser in the first verse of this passage. The relationship between The Vine and The Vinedresser is clear here, and digging into it is critical to understanding our relationship to The Vine, who is The Vinedresser's Son.

The true Vine has an intimate relationship with His Father, The Vinedresser. The relationship of Father to Son and Son to Father has profound meaning as we ponder our relationship to the triune God as well as the triune God's relationship to us. We pause at the foot of The Vine as He articulates His relationship to His Father and His Father's relationship to Him.

In the 21st century, being a vinedresser is considered a high position, perhaps even a romantic position. This may be because of the grape grower's close relationship to the land and to the wine that sustainable farming produces. People are hungry to know where their food and wine come from; they want to be close to the land and the soil because they want to know their own roots. People love meeting my father because they want to know a vinedresser and to hear stories from his labor of love.

In Jesus' day, being a vinedresser was not a high position, and Jesus calling His heavenly Father The Vinedresser would have raised eyebrows. In the Old Testament, a vinedresser, also known as a soil worker, was a poor person who worked the land. Consider these examples:

- Zechariah prophesied that a fountain of God would open up to cleanse the people and that the vinedressers who had prophesied falsely would say, "I am no prophet, I am a worker of the soil, for a man sold me in my youth" (Zechariah 13:5).

- God worked through King Nebuchadnezzar to bring punishment on the rebellious children of Israel. Jerusalem was destroyed and almost all of the people were dragged off into captivity. The poorest were left behind to be vinedressers and farmers (2 Kings 25:11–12; Jeremiah 52:12–16).

Jesus' statement—My Father is The Vinedresser—were humble words with profound meaning. They were spoken in the Upper Room as Jesus, the Lamb of God, prepared to face the cross to spill His lifeblood. He knew that He would be placed in the soil, in the grave. Jesus submitted to His Father's will; Jesus fulfilled all righteousness; Jesus would die and be buried in the soil; Jesus would come forth from the grave into resurrection glory by the working of The Vinedresser's mighty hand.

Jesus' words speak of an intimate relationship between Father and Son, a very important concept as we listen to The Vine speak. John's Gospel provides a wealth of examples of Jesus' relationship with His Father. At times, as He articulated that relationship, Jesus spoke words of comfort to His followers. At times, His words were painfully harsh as He called stubborn religious leaders to wake up to His Father's work. Jesus' words created energy and life. His words also fueled the energy of hatred as He proclaimed Himself one with the Father, His word and work as one with the Father.

Jesus' word and work were then and are now a call into the life of the true Vine and to submission to the work of The Vinedresser. John's Gospel records a profound journey of the Word of life, Jesus, who by His Word called His followers and, in that call, created faith and desire in their hearts. Consider these examples of Jesus spending His energy to nurture life:

- Jesus turned water into the best wine ever made.

- Jesus called Nicodemus into faith in the triune God.

- Jesus interacted with the lowly woman at the well and declared Himself to be "the living water" (John 4:1–42).

John listened to and watched Jesus' word and work. He deeply desired that his readers understand The Vine's relationship with The Vinedresser. John records:

> So Jesus said to them, "Truly, truly, I say to you, the Son can do nothing of His own accord, but only what He sees the Father doing. For whatever the Father does, that the Son does likewise. For the Father loves the Son and shows Him all that He Himself is doing. And greater works than these will He show Him, so that you may marvel. For as the Father raises the dead and gives them life, so also the Son gives life to whom He will." (John 5:19–21)

As Jesus worked and spoke, the controversy surrounding Him intensified. Consider the verses immediately before the preceding passage:

> And this was why the Jews were persecuting Jesus, because He was doing these things on the Sabbath. But Jesus answered them, "My Father is working until now, and I am working." This was why the Jews were seeking all the more to kill Him, because not only was He breaking the Sabbath, but He was even calling God His own Father, making Himself equal with God. (John 5:16–18)

Jesus spoke these words to religious leaders in the presence of His disciples and other followers. There was a widening gap between the faith of the followers and the rejection of Jesus' words by the religious leaders. There was also a very noticeable difference in the energy of those surrounding Jesus. Those who believed Him lived the energy of hope; those who rejected Jesus lived the energy of hatred and death.

Jesus watched His Father work; Jesus worked that work. We ascribe the work of creation to the work of God the Father, but Jesus' words call us to think differently, to think more. The Son watches the Father work, and He works that same work. Jesus' Word worked faith and exhibited power and control over creation. He calmed storms, healed the lame, and fed the multitudes. The Vinedresser works and the true Vine works that same work to bring life and growth and health and fruit.

His disciples' response to Jesus' conversation with religious leaders led them to ask about doing the work of God: "Then they said to Him, 'What must we do, to be doing the works of God?' Jesus answered them, 'This is the work of God, that you believe in Him whom He has sent'" (John 6:28–29). They asked, "What do we have to do in order to do God's work?" Jesus said that they were to receive God's work and His work, which created faith in them.

John records more of The Vine's teaching about His relationship with The Vinedresser. Consider these energy-filled, life-filled events:

- Jesus raised Lazarus by calling him forth, and He healed the man born blind.

- Jesus declared "I am the Good Shepherd" and "I am the resurrection and the life."

- Jesus foretold His arrest and crucifixion, and He washed the disciples' feet.

- Jesus also declared "Let not your hearts be troubled" and "I am the way, the truth, and the life. No one comes to the Father except through Me."

Jesus' interaction with Philip is critically important to our study of the relationship between The Vine and The Vinedresser. These verses call us to believe in the oneness of the Father and Son. Jesus also says to believe His Word. But if that is too much, at least believe in Him because of the work He does. These verses have been formative in my understanding of The Vine and His word and work for us and in us and through us. Jesus said:

> "If you had known Me, you would have known My Father also. From now on you do know Him and have seen Him." Philip said to Him, "Lord, show us the Father, and it is enough for us." Jesus said to him, "Have I been with you so long, and you still do not know Me, Philip? Whoever has seen Me has seen the Father. How can you say, 'Show us the Father'? Do you not believe that I am in the Father and the Father is in Me? The words that I say to you I do not speak on My own authority, but the Father who dwells in Me does His works. Believe Me that I am in the Father and the Father is in Me, or else believe on account of the works themselves." (John 14:7–11)

The Vine had His face set on the cross and the resurrection as He spoke these words. The Vine spoke comfort as He continued to work His work through His Word in the hearts and minds of the disciples. Up to this point, they had witnessed His word and work; soon, they would witness His death. They would also witness His life burst forth from the grave.

The Vine speaks relationship—He is in the Father, we are in Him, He is in us. Jesus continued:

> I will ask the Father, and He will give you another Helper, to be with you forever, even the Spirit of truth, whom the world cannot receive, because it neither sees Him nor

knows Him. You know Him, for He dwells with you and will be in you.

I will not leave you as orphans; I will come to you. Yet a little while and the world will see Me no more, but you will see Me. Because I live, you also will live. In that day you will know that I am in My Father, and you in Me, and I in you. (John 14:16–20)

These words are astounding, awe-inspiring, and breathtaking. The Vinedresser, The Vine, and The Spirit of The Vine work together to call, create, restore, heal, and calm. The triune God provides us a life-giving, holy place to dwell, and He also dwells in us. The Vine doesn't work in us from a distance, but rather from a flesh-on-flesh, "grafted-in" relationship.

THE VINEDRESSER SPEAKS:
GOD'S WORD FROM THE OLD TESTAMENT

For a proper context in this study, we must also dig deeper into the words of The Vinedresser in relationship to The Vine in the Old Testament. The Old Testament contains rich language of vine and vineyard. There were instructions for planting a vineyard, including how wide to plant rows. There were instructions about not pruning vines or gathering fruit during the Year of Jubilee. There was a law stating that you could eat fruit from someone else's vineyard but not put their grapes into your bag.

There were also words of destruction and of healing using vineyard imagery. The psalmist spoke the words of The Vinedresser as he looked forward to the life of The Vine:

You brought a vine out of Egypt; You drove out the nations and planted it. You cleared the ground for it; it took deep root and filled the land. The mountains were covered with its shade, the mighty cedars with its branches. It sent out its branches to the sea and its shoots to the River. Why then have You broken down its walls, so that all who pass along the way pluck its fruit? The boar from the forest ravages it, and all that move in the field feed on it.

Turn again, O God of hosts! Look down from heaven, and see; have regard for this vine, the stock that Your right hand planted, and for the son whom You made strong for Yourself. They have burned it with fire; they have cut it down; may they perish at the rebuke of Your face! But let Your hand be on the man of Your right hand, the son of man whom You have made strong for Yourself! Then we shall not turn back from You; give us life, and we will call upon Your name!

Restore us, O Lord God of hosts! Let Your face shine, that we may be saved! (Psalm 80:8–19)

The prophet Amos spoke The Vinedresser's wrath using vineyard language:

Therefore because you trample on the poor and you exact taxes of grain from him, you have built houses of hewn stone, but you shall not dwell in them; you have planted pleasant vineyards, but you shall not drink their wine. For I know how many are your transgressions and how great are your sins—you who afflict the righteous, who take a bribe, and turn aside the needy in the gate. Therefore he who is prudent will keep silent in such a time, for it is an evil time. (Amos 5:11–13)

Amos also spoke The Vinedresser's promise of restoration and healing on the people using vineyard language:

> "I will restore the fortunes of My people Israel, and they shall rebuild the ruined cities and inhabit them; they shall plant vineyards and drink their wine, and they shall make gardens and eat their fruit. I will plant them on their land, and they shall never again be uprooted out of the land that I have given them," says the LORD your God. (Amos 9:14–15)

In addition to vineyard language, it is critical to look at the Old Testament work of The Vinedresser, calling and restoring and pointing people to His promise of life in The Vine. My father's work in our family's vineyard is hands-on; it is constant and consistent. His work is always done for the health and growth and life and fruit of the vines. Keep in mind the vinedresser's work as you ponder these words from the Old Testament about the work of God.

The religious leaders of Jesus' day claimed Moses as their father. Here are God's words through Moses about the work of God, The Vinedresser:

- In the beginning, God created the heavens and the earth. The earth was without form and void, and darkness was over the face of the deep. And the Spirit of God was hovering over the face of the waters. And God said, "Let there be light," and there was light. (Genesis 1:1–3)

- Then Moses turned and went down from the mountain with the two tablets of the testimony in his hand, tablets that were written on both sides; on the front and on the back they were written. The tablets were the work of God, and the writing was the writing of God, engraved on the tablets. (Exodus 32:15–16)

- See now that I, even I, am He, and there is no god beside Me; I kill and I make alive; I wound and I heal; and there is none that can deliver out of My hand. (Deuteronomy 32:39)

The Psalms reflect faith in the powerful word and work of God:

- Summon Your power, O God, the power, O God, by which You have worked for us. (Psalm 68:28)

- Yet God my King is from of old, working salvation in the midst of the earth. (Psalm 74:12)

Luke records that when Jesus began His public ministry, He stood in the midst of people in the synagogue and quoted Isaiah:

The Spirit of the Lord is upon Me, because He has anointed Me to proclaim good news to the poor. He has sent Me to proclaim liberty to the captives and recovering of sight to the blind, to set at liberty those who are oppressed, to proclaim the year of the Lord's favor. (Luke 4:18–19)

Luke tells us that in this moment, Jesus was the center of attention among His followers and the religious leaders in the synagogue. He was formally proclaiming His relationship to God the Father, to The Vinedresser. And in so doing, He challenged the religious leaders that if they believed Moses, then they would believe Him (John 5).

THE BRANCHES SPEAK: THE APOSTLES' WORDS

The Vinedresser and The Vine have spoken. The branches, the apostles, heard their words and followed their call. The word and work of The Vinedresser and The Vine permeated their being. Christ's energy and life flowed into every cell. Having heard, they spoke. The word and work of

The Vinedresser in and through the life of The Vine worked then and is at work now.

We have heard The Vine speak; we have heard The Vinedresser speak. The apostles are branches of The Vine, and they have much to say about the work of God the Father, The Vinedresser. Think about Paul's understanding of the powerful work of God from the context of The Vine, The Vinedresser, and the grafted-in branches of The Vine:

- Of this gospel I was made a minister according to the gift of God's grace, which was given me by the working of His power. (Ephesians 3:7)

- For it is God who works in you, both to will and to work for His good pleasure. (Philippians 2:13)

- And we also thank God constantly for this, that when you received the word of God, which you heard from us, you accepted it not as the word of men but as what it really is, the word of God, which is at work in you believers. (1 Thessalonians 2:13)

Paul's language places the word and work of God together as two aspects of the same thing. The Vinedresser and The Vine work through their word and work to work their work. This sounds redundant, but isn't. The Vine, into whom we are grafted, is always at work. The roots and the flow of the sap bring forth growth and health and fruit. Paul's words to the Church of Colossae help us understand our grafted-in relationship as well as the power of God at work in us:

Therefore, as you received Christ Jesus the Lord, so walk in Him, rooted and built up in Him and established in the faith, just as you were taught, abounding in thanksgiving.

See to it that no one takes you captive by philosophy and

empty deceit, according to human tradition, according to the elemental spirits of the world, and not according to Christ. For in Him the whole fullness of deity dwells bodily, and you have been filled in Him, who is the head of all rule and authority. In Him also you were circumcised with a circumcision made without hands, by putting off the body of the flesh, by the circumcision of Christ, having been buried with Him in baptism, in which you were also raised with Him through faith in the powerful working of God, who raised Him from the dead. (Colossians 2:6–12)

THE BRANCHES SPEAK: MY STORY

My father works hard to accomplish all of the tasks associated with farming a large family vineyard. In addition to all of the vinedresser's tasks and responsibilities previously listed, he also fixes equipment, caters meals with my mom, and serves on various committees. He always lends a hand in the tasting room, telling stories, posing for photos, or signing wine bottles. He's one of the grandfathers in the modern era of vineyards in Paso Robles, California.

Many visitors and friends thank me for sharing my dad with them because he reminds them so much of their father or grandfather or uncle. Dad is quick to put his arm around someone (including me). He gets choked up when he speaks his heart or prays for our family around the dinner table. He took my son under his wing before he could walk, and now my son is learning what his grandpa knows about life and vineyards and farming. My son mirrors my father's work ethic.

It is easy to visit the vineyard and see only beauty and perfection. But the vinedresser doesn't see it that way. Dad sees beauty, of course, but he also looks for problems to solve, identifies what work needs to take place,

My Father and His Mother

orders it done, and oversees the work. Dad takes care of the vines. I'm not idolizing him or making him larger than life, but his work helps me see the magnificence and variety of God's work.

My father is the vinedresser. My son and I watch his work because one day, we will work as the vinedressers of our vineyards. God is the perfect vinedresser. Jesus watched His Father work, and He worked those works. God's will and His Word and His work always have been in the very best interest of the branches.

When I speak about our family history or on behalf of our family's vineyards and winery, I am speaking my father's heart. I am also speaking my mother's heart, as she is actively involved in the family business as well. When Jesus spoke, He spoke His Father's heart and His Father's will. My father's words give direction to bring growth and health and life and fruit to the vines. Jesus' words take effect to bring life and growth and health and fruit to us.

We have been raised by earthly fathers, which means there may be significant challenges to our believing in God as the vinedresser and seeing His work in our lives. (For example, those who were raised in neglectful or abusive homes may be challenged by the concept of God as a good, heavenly Father.) Such challenges may get in the way of our growing in The Vine if they are not identified and acknowledged and processed. This study isn't the place for that kind of exploration, but it may serve as a starting point. Professional and pastoral help are valuable tools if the pain of our earthly relationships gets in the way of grasping hold of the beauty of God's Word.

I am blessed to have a close working relationship with my father, but it has not been without struggles. My father is a hard worker of German Lutheran heritage. Emotions and talking and interpreting and filtering and growing and feeling were secondary to his providing for our family of six. My father has changed a lot since I was a child. Showing his emotions comes much more easily as he has matured and continues to grow in The Vine. Still, phrases he used and messages he communicated during my childhood stick in the very fiber of my being and cause me to think and feel things about myself and about God that simply aren't true:

- Quit your crying, or I'll give you something to cry about.
- Shape up!
- Anger is wrong!
- Get to work!
- If we don't talk about hard topics, they will go away.

Identifying those things and overcoming them has helped me mature in my relationship with my father and with God the Father as I have grown in The Vine. The job God gives parents is to raise children in His way. His way, His created, beautiful way, is to nurture the whole being: body, heart, mind, soul, and spirit. Knowledge and work ethic without emotions and

Father and Daughter

feelings are meaningless; emotions and feelings without knowledge and work ethic are meaningless. Integrating all aspects is one of the greatest challenges of parenting. Children must be guided to grow in understanding of their emotions (anger being one of the most powerful).

Every individual has the responsibility to ask, "How has my relationship with my earthly father impacted my understanding of my heavenly Father's work for me and in me?" My answer is that my relationship with my father (and with my mother) has had a profound impact on my choices and on how I view God's word and work. A Christian therapist has helped me interpret how and what I learned during my childhood and understand that my learning has been on a cellular level. He also helped me interpret that my childhood led to the choices I made as an adult. Taking responsibility for my growth (not blaming anyone for anything) has been my goal of learning to interpret. Here are some examples:

- I remained silent.

- I worked so hard to make something good.

- I didn't get angry when anger was appropriate.

- I didn't say "Ouch!" when I hurt.

If they are not identified and replaced with The Vinedresser and The Vine's words of mercy and healing, then false or hurtful messages become louder and louder. Working through the work of the relationship of The Vinedresser to The Vine and to the branches can be difficult if pain from our childhood is in the way. God calls us to wrestle with hard issues so we grow in The Vine. God works in us and for us; God works in us so He can work through us as His authentic, genuine people.

Jesus is the true Vine and His Father is The Vinedresser. Their relationship has profound meaning as it relates to our relationship to the triune God and His work for us and in us. Jesus watched His Father's work, and He worked. To mimic our own father's work may not be beneficial in every way. However, watching and mimicking God's work and the work of His Son is our high and holy calling as His children, as branches in The Vine.

The Branches Speak: Your Story

Discuss the following questions with your small group with the understanding that what is shared is to be kept among the group. Please be sensitive to people in your group who may have been hurt deeply by a father or father figure (or mother). Don't pretend you know their pain. Share only as much as you feel comfortable sharing. Share more with your pastor or with a trusted professional. Share more with God in prayer.

1. What has The Vine spoken to your heart today?
2. What aspects of your father's relationship with you help you see Jesus' relationship with His Father and His relationship with you more clearly?

3. What aspects of your father's relationship with you create a stumbling block to seeing your relationship with God and His relationship with you?

4. Which verses stand out and give you courage and hope?

Chapter Six

Training the Branches

The Vine Speaks: My Father's Vineyard

Training the branches of the vine is a three-year process. The trellis system, which is built before the vines are planted, is crucial. The trellis system gives uniformity and structure to the vines and to the vineyard as a whole. The steel post and wire system provides stability as well as freedom for the branches of the vine to grow and produce fruit. Training also optimizes productivity and quality.

Before new vines are planted in freshly prepared soil, a grid is created. Our vineyard hires an irrigation company to design an irrigation field plan, which is like a set of house plans. From the plan, they use GPS to create a large grid in the empty field. Then they use the grid markers to place mainlines, submains, and risers for the drip irrigation system. We use these same grid markers to carefully mark ten-foot row spacing and six-foot spaces between vines.

Building the trellis involves marking the field with plastic table knives, laying out metal training stakes, and pounding them into the soil at precise spots. Large end posts are pounded deeply into the ground to anchor the end of each row. Wire is rolled out, tied to the end posts, and clipped to the steel stakes. Irrigation drip hose is clipped to the lowest hanging wire. The trellis system takes months to build, but it must be constructed before the vines are planted.

We plant the little potted vines in a uniform, very precise manner, three inches west of the stake. My father supervises, making sure the vines are planted in the correct place. A training tube is placed over the young vines to protect them from creatures that would eat the supple leaves. This training tube also has a greenhouse effect, making water use very efficient. The tube causes the vine to grow upward rather than out. The green leaves push to the top of the tube quickly, giving us a long branch.

The first little branch that grows from the graft union is loosely tied to the vertical stake and becomes the trunk of the vine. The trunk stays in place for the life of the vine. When branches grow tall enough to reach the horizontal wire of the trellis system, they are all loosely tied to the wire so they angle in the same direction.

The vines are continually assessed and trained. As the vine grows, another new branch is trained to the wire in the opposite direction to form a bilateral system.

Training the vines on the trellis system is a delicate process. The branches are loosely wrapped around the wire with stretchy tie tape that is loose enough to leave room for growth and movement. The tie tape must be tied around the branch and the wire firmly enough to keep the branches on the wire but not so tight as to restrict sap flow. Branches remain tied to the stake and wire for the life of the plant. After the first year, we call the branch on the stake "the trunk" and the branches on the wire "the cordon."

Soil Preparation

Training

Training the vines to the stake and wire of the trellis system keeps the vines stable for the work of bearing fruit for the entire life of the vine. It also provides uniformity in the vineyard, which is important for the work we accomplish. The structure provides freedom to grow and bear fruit.

The trellis system to which the vines are trained is imperative as the vines cannot bear the weight of the fruit they produce without it. But young branches strain against the system, preferring freedom to grow freely. As the vines mature, the cordon grows around the wire. The supple tendrils that grow at intervals among the leaves wrap themselves around the trellis, adding one more layer of structure so that the vines can grow freely and easily handle the weight of the branches and fruit.

THE VINE SPEAKS: JESUS' WORDS

I am the true vine, and My Father is the vinedresser. Every branch in Me that does not bear fruit He takes away, and every branch that does bear fruit He prunes, that it may bear more fruit. Already you are clean because of the word that I

have spoken to you. Abide in Me, and I in you. As the branch cannot bear fruit by itself, unless it abides in the vine, neither can you, unless you abide in Me. I am the vine; you are the branches. Whoever abides in Me and I in him, he it is that bears much fruit, for apart from Me you can do nothing. . . .

If you keep My commandments, you will abide in My love, just as I have kept My Father's commandments and abide in His love. These things I have spoken to you, that My joy may be in you, and that your joy may be full. (John 15: 1–5, 10–11)

Jesus' word and work trained those who had ears to hear and eyes to see that He was the Son of the living God. The word Jesus used in Luke 6:40, when He said, "A disciple is not above his teacher, but everyone when he is fully trained will be like his teacher," is the Greek word *kataritzō*. The fundamental meaning is "to put a thing in its appropriate position, to establish, to set up, to equip, to instruct fully." The Vine speaks the call. His desire was to train up His disciples.

Jesus called out to the Twelve, "Follow Me." The true Vine spoke in that call, and His word worked faith, desire, and ability to be trained by the Creator. Those who are trained in the things of God are trained in theology. In Jesus' day, students chose a master teacher to study under. In the modern day, we choose a university and professors to study under.

Jesus' call to follow Him turned religious tradition upside down. His calling of and subsequent training of the motley group of twelve was a call to focus entirely on His word and work, to grow up in His life, to be witnesses, to receive. Jesus' call and training was and is based entirely on an intimate relationship to, with, and in The Vine. Everything God ever demanded, He provided in the life of His Son, who said, "I am the true vine, and My Father is the vinedresser. Abide in Me."

Training up the branches of the vine onto the wire trellis system gives the branches stability and structure. I use the language "train up" and "grow up" intentionally. The roots grow down; the branches are trained up on the structure and grow up toward light. The trellis system provides structure so that growth and fruit production can be achieved. Far from restricting, the structure gives freedom to bear fruit. I view the trellis system as the Law of God in our lives.

The Law provides structure and stability within the training system, that is, within life on this earth. Jesus came to fulfill the Law, which gives us freedom from the Law. Jesus came to train, to position, to call disciples to be witnesses of His word and work. His word and work do the same for us today. His fulfillment of the Law freed us from the condemnation of the Law, and the Law provides structure for freedom to grow and bear His fruit.

Jesus' training up of His followers had roots in a new command, which wasn't new. Jesus said, "A new commandment I give to you, that you love one another: just as I have loved you, you also are to love one another. By this all people will know that you are My disciples, if you have love for one another" (John 13:34–35). Jesus quotes the summary of all Old Testament Law to the confused teachers of the Law:

> But when the Pharisees heard that He had silenced the Sadducees, they gathered together. And one of them, a lawyer, asked Him a question to test Him. "Teacher, which is the great commandment in the Law?" And He said to him, "You shall love the Lord your God with all your heart and with all your soul and with all your mind. This is the great and first commandment. And a second is like it: You shall love your neighbor as yourself. On these two com- mandments depend all the Law and the Prophets." (Mat- thew 22:34–40)

Jesus commanded that His followers keep His commandments: "If you keep My commandments, you will abide in My love, just as I have kept My Father's commandments and abide in His love. These things I have spoken to you, that My joy may be in you, and that your joy may be full" (John 15:10–11). The command to "keep" the commandments has always been grounded in God's call to be His people. "Keeping the com- mandments" is grounded in The Vine's life, in His call to abide in Him, and in the training to be His people.

Jesus' call and training had another effect: it revealed the deep hatred and confusion at work in the hearts of the religious leaders of the day. They wanted to train Jesus to their ways. They wanted Jesus to "keep" as they interpreted God's command to "keep." They wanted and tried with their whole beings to restrain Jesus' word and work.

Jesus' call and training created faith and a desire to grow up and be further trained up in The Vine. John recorded Jesus' words "I am the vine, abide in Me" in the heart of his Gospel. Jesus' demand to "keep His commands," these training words in this study of the Vine and the branches, must not be taken out of context. To do so would be like being trained in Old Testament Law outside the context of God's declaration "Fear not, for I have redeemed you; I have called you by name, you are Mine" (Isaiah 43:1).

Jesus' words in the chapters surrounding His "I am the vine" declaration are critical to our understanding of being trained up in The Vine. John's record of the events and training words in John 13–17 take place after Jesus entered Jerusalem to face death on the cross. Jesus knew that suffering and death were coming, and He turned toward it. Jesus foretold His own death, served His Last Supper, announced that someone would betray Him, dismissed Judas, and washed the disciples' feet.

After those words and events, Jesus said, "A new commandment I give to you, that you love one another: just as I have loved you, you also are to love one another. By this all people will know that you are My disciples, if you have love for one another" (John 13:34–35). Jesus loved Himself, God, and us, and He kept God's commands with His life.

- The Vine gives a new command to love.
- The Vine is the new covenant.
- The Vine kept the old covenant perfectly.

The command to love is new because Jesus is new. The command is new because our relationship to God is new in the life of The Vine. All focus must be on His life and relationship to us and with us and in us. Confusing the old and new covenants would be like confusing the trellising system with the freedom it provides the branches of the vine to bear fruit.

Jesus' words are His call, and His training in our lives flows from His life. These words call and equip and position us in His life. Everything God demands, He provides. He commands love; He is love. He creates; He re-creates. His life breeds life, and His life breeds love. We live in The Vine, and He dwells in us. His life flows in us, and His life flows through us. From the context of these words, "Let not your heart be troubled; believe in God, believe also in Me," Jesus says:

> Truly, truly, I say to you, whoever believes in Me will also do the works that I do; and greater works than these will he do, because I am going to the Father. Whatever you ask in My name, this I will do, that the Father may be glorified in the Son. If you ask Me anything in My name, I will do it. If you love Me, you will keep My commandments. And I will ask the Father, and He will give you another Helper, to be with you forever, even the Spirit of truth, whom the world cannot receive, because it neither sees Him nor knows Him. You know Him, for He dwells with you and will be in you. I will not leave you as orphans; I will come to you. Yet a little while and the world will see Me no more, but you will see Me. Because I live, you also will live. In that day you will know that I am in My Father, and you in Me, and I in you. Whoever has My commandments and keeps them, he it is who loves Me. And he who loves Me will be loved by My Father, and I will love him and manifest Myself to him." (John 14:12–21)

Jesus' command, if taken out of context, could cause us to focus on the training system instead of on the freedom and life in Him. If the branches of the vine wind too tightly around the training wire or are tied too tightly to the wire, they are constricted. The lifeblood of the vine, the sap, cannot flow past the point of constriction. If we are tied too tightly to the Law, our lives are constricted and the lifeblood of The Vine cannot flow freely.

The Vine calls us, trains us deeper into His holy life, and provides freedom to bear fruit in His life. The Law, which Jesus fulfilled perfectly, provides structure and stability. It also provides freedom to bear fruit where we're called to bear fruit. The Law does not bind or constrict. The Law does not hold us captive. It cannot and does not condemn us. The Vine fulfilled all righteousness and is our righteousness. His life provides a home as we abide in Him and He in us. The Vine breeds life and freedom and growth.

Look at these verses from John 14 again. As you read, pay attention to words like "believe," "do," "keep," "love," and "ask." Note phrases that reflect Jesus' action toward us: "I have loved you"; "I will ask the Father"; "He will give you another Helper, to be with you forever"; "I will come to you"; "I live"; "I am in my Father, and you in Me, and I in you."

We are called to pause in the words The Vine speaks and ask for discernment and wisdom. Digesting these words requires time, a deep breath, and prayer for courage to grasp their richness. Jesus trains us up to receive His word and work on a cellular level, in the fiber of our being. Our hearts pump blood to every cell of our body to cleanse and renew. Jesus' heart pumps His body and blood into every cell of our being. He cleanses, renews, and purifies, giving life and growth and freedom in and through His life.

Jesus continued training as He spoke a very vivid picture of abiding in the vine and drawing life from His life, energy from His energy. Jesus said, "If you keep My commandments, you will abide in My love, just as I have kept My Father's commandments and abide in His love. These things I have spoken to you, that My joy may be in you, and that your joy may be full" (John 15:10–11). Jesus' call to keep and abide is accomplished in our life, which is lived in His life. This is not a rigid, suffocating demand to do what He has already done. This is a joy-filled activity of life, of growing and bearing fruit that flows naturally from life in The Vine.

Jesus spoke these words as part of training the disciples for what was to come in His suffering, death, and resurrection. John recalled and recorded these words sixty years later, that "[we] may believe . . . and that by believing [we] may have life in His name" (John 20:3). Jesus' training words don't throw us deeper into the Law. Jesus' words breed life and growth and love as we trust His life for us. We bow to The Vine's word and work for us and in us. He provides us a dwelling place in His life, and He lives His life in us.

THE BRANCHES SPEAK: THE APOSTLES' WORDS

The apostles were trained up as branches in The Vine. They witnessed love in action and were called to the new command by Jesus' word and work. They wrestled with the meaning of the words *abide, dwell, keep, love,* and *ask.* The apostles trusted Jesus despite their fears and failures. He continually and patiently called them to focus on His word and work.

The words the apostles speak as branches in The Vine guide us today into a deeper understanding of being trained up. Their words are the Word of God, calling us and training us to grow and live and bear fruit. Because we live in this earthly world, our ears have been trained to listen to the binding words of the world: what we have done wrong or that we *are* wrong. But we are called by Christ to listen to His freeing words and to be trained up in freedom to grow and bear fruit. The Law provides structure so we can grow and bear fruit.

Paul had been trained according to the finest Jewish traditions. He was passionate and powerful as he sought to wipe out the movement to follow the crucified Son of a carpenter. But Paul's training was turned upside down when The Vine called him from hate and murder to truth and love. Paul's thoughtful words call us deeper into Jesus' new command to love:

- Now before faith came, we were held captive under the law, imprisoned until the coming faith would be revealed. So then, the law was our guardian until Christ came, in order that we might be justified by faith. But now that faith has come, we are no longer under a guardian, for in Christ Jesus you are all sons of God, through faith. For as many of you as were baptized into Christ have put on Christ. There is neither Jew nor Greek, there is neither slave nor free, there is no male and female, for you are all one in Christ Jesus. And if you are Christ's, then you are Abraham's offspring, heirs according to promise. (Galatians 3:23–29)

- For freedom Christ has set us free; stand firm therefore, and do not submit again to a yoke of slavery. . . . For you were called to freedom, brothers. Only do not use your freedom as an opportunity for the flesh, but through love serve one another. For the whole law is fulfilled in one word: "You shall love your neighbor as yourself." (Galatians 5:1, 13–14)

- Brothers, if anyone is caught in any transgression, you who are spiritual should restore him in a spirit of gentleness. Keep watch on yourself, lest you too be tempted. Bear one another's burdens, and so fulfill the law of Christ. For if anyone thinks he is something, when he is nothing, he deceives himself. But let each one test his own work, and then his reason to boast will be in himself alone and not in his neighbor. For each will have to bear his own load. (Galatians 6:1–5) (For more on passage, read *Boundaries* by Henry Cloud and John Townsend.)

- Since we have such a hope, we are very bold, not like Moses, who would put a veil over his face so that the Israelites might not gaze at the outcome of what was being brought to an end. But their minds were hardened. For to this day, when they read the old covenant, that same veil remains un-lifted, because only through Christ is it taken away. Yes, to this day whenever Moses is read a veil lies over their hearts. But when one turns to the Lord, the veil is removed. Now the Lord is the Spirit, and where the Spirit of the Lord is, there is freedom. And we all, with unveiled face, beholding the glory of the Lord, are being transformed into the same image from one degree of glory to another. For this comes from the Lord who is the Spirit. (2 Corinthians 3:12–18)

John followed Jesus' call and was trained up as a branch in The Vine. Having received Jesus' word and work as a branch in The Vine, John spoke and wrote. John's words are for us that we, too, might be trained up in The Vine. John speaks the truth in love when he says, "If we don't love, we are not walking in the light; if we love, we walk in light" (see 1 John 1:5–10). He calls branches of The Vine to know that in love, there is perfect free-dom and, conversely, that in fear, there is no freedom. Take time to digest these training words:

- Beloved, let us love one another, for love is from God, and whoever loves has been born of God and knows God. Any-one who does not love does not know God, because God is love. In this the love of God was made manifest among us, that God sent His only Son into the world, so that we might live through Him. In this is love, not that we have loved God but that He loved us and sent His Son to be the propitiation for our sins. Beloved, if God so loved us, we also ought to love one another. No one has ever seen God; if we love one another, God abides in us and His love is perfected in us.

  By this we know that we abide in Him and He in us, because He has given us of His Spirit. And we have seen and tes-tify that the Father has sent His Son to be the Savior of the world. Whoever confesses that Jesus is the Son of God, God abides in him, and he in God. So we have come to know and to believe the love that God has for us. God is love, and whoever abides in love abides in God, and God abides in him. By this is love perfected with us, so that we may have confidence for the day of judgment, because as He is so also are we in this world. There is no fear in love, but perfect love casts out fear. For fear has to do with punishment, and whoever fears has not been perfected in love. We love because He first loved us. If anyone says, "I love God," and hates his brother, he is a liar; for he who does not love his brother whom he has seen cannot love God whom he has not seen. And this commandment we have from Him: whoever loves God must also love his brother. (1 John 4:7–21)

- Everyone who believes that Jesus is the Christ has been born of God, and everyone who loves the Father loves whoever has been born of Him. By this we know that we love the children of God, when we love God and obey His commandments. For this is the love of God, that we keep His commandments. And His commandments are not burdensome. For everyone who has been born of God overcomes the world. And this is the victory that has overcome the world—our faith. Who is it that overcomes the world except the one who believes that Jesus is the Son of God? (1 John 5:1–5)

- I rejoiced greatly to find some of your children walking in the truth, just as we were commanded by the Father. And now I ask you, dear lady—not as though I were writing you a new commandment, but the one we have had from the beginning—that we love one another. And this is love, that we walk according to His commandments; this is the commandment, just as you have heard from the beginning, so that you should walk in it. (2 John 1:4–6)

Peter's training in Christ was an intriguing journey that provides rich examples for our training and faith life. Jesus stopped the outspoken fisherman with His training words. Peter wanted to train Jesus and direct His word and work, but that was not Jesus' call. As is the case for many of us, Peter learned the hard way about life in The Vine. But learn he did, and now, as a branch in The Vine, he speaks:

- For this is the will of God, that by doing good you should put to silence the ignorance of foolish people. Live as people who are free, not using your freedom as a cover-up for evil, but living as servants of God. Honor everyone. Love the brotherhood. Fear God. Honor the emperor. (1 Peter 2:15–17)

- He himself bore our sins in His body on the tree, that we might die to sin and live to righteousness. By His wounds you have been healed. For you were straying like sheep, but have now returned to the Shepherd and Overseer of your souls. (1 Peter 2:24–25)

- Above all, keep loving one another earnestly, since love covers a multitude of sins. Show hospitality to one another without grumbling. (1 Peter 4:8–9)

THE BRANCHES SPEAK: MY STORY

Training me up as a child could not have been easy for my parents, who had been blessed with the birth of my brother just eleven months before I was born. I was a busy child, always ready for the next adventure. I was a morally aware child with a deep desire to do the right thing, and I wanted to do it at warp speed. I learned early the words "I'll do it by myself."

I challenged my parents by giving them many opportunities to discipline me. I wasn't bad, just busy. I also wanted to talk about everything in depth. I needed to know why. I wanted to know about the soul. I needed to know what love really was. I was told not to get angry because anger was wrong. I felt angry sometimes and felt horribly wrong because I felt anger. I wanted to know about anger and love. I learned to be sufficient on my own and resigned myself to finding answers on my own.

Constantly on the move on large acreage, I was always testing boundaries and, of course, testing my parents' patience. I was an explorer and a wanderer. Getting cut and needing stitches was a common event. My earliest memory of an injury was as a three-year-old. I was "helping" Dad when I fell into a well. I vaguely remember the trip to the doctor and stitches in my bottom lip. I remember another trip to the hospital to sew up a gaping hole in my chest caused by a go-cart crash. I wrestled with the environment and my physicality.

I also wrestled with spiritual and faith contradictions. I was being trained in the ways of God by pastors who talked about love but didn't act loving. I was told that forgiveness is important, but I watched as families didn't forgive. I was told that gossip was wrong, but I overheard adults discuss actions people took, clothing people wore, or private details of the lives of others. I heard people say "speak the truth in love," but the hard things were never talked about. When challenging topics were broached, it wasn't in a loving, training way.

My upbringing, coupled with many emotional injuries and the unfinished healing process of those injuries, led to denying pain. I believed that not saying "Ouch!" when I hurt was a badge of honor.

Together with a lack of boundaries and a longing to have my soul fed and to be loved for being me, these contradictions gave rise to conflicts in my young mind, and I turned to self-training. I determined to do it myself. I would feed my own spirit.

Marriage and children had always been my desire, so I set out to find a spouse. But I embarked on dating and romance with an underdeveloped emotional and spiritual well-being and the habit of denying physical and emotional pain. Looking back, I can see that I was ill equipped to choose a life partner. I can also see that there were many signs of an unhealthy relationship, but I didn't want to see or feel them. For example, now I see that I didn't know how to distinguish healthy anger from unhealthy anger. When my future husband and I were dating, angry outbursts occurred. When they did, I was startled and embarrassed. I was scared and hurt. I hadn't been raised in a home where anger was expressed. I was ill equipped to recognize my own fear or pain, so I didn't recognize the danger of explosive anger. I had been taught to love and not be angry, so I spoke about loving and not being angry. I resigned myself to unhealthy responses and actions so he wouldn't get angry.

I was being trained up. I apologized regularly for my improper behavior and promised I would be more careful with my actions. I began watching my behavior closely so I wouldn't make him angry, and I tried to do my best to keep everything in order in our home. I tried to mitigate every possible opportunity for an angry explosion, and I failed regularly. I thought if I loved him more, he would surely love me back and be nice, consistently.

My training in the Word of God taught me to love and to carry one another's burdens and to fulfill the Law of Christ. My boundaries weakened with every angry explosion, and I carried his burdens and mine. While strong and confident to the outside world, inside I was a little child crying for the Word of God to touch my life so I could be a better, more beautiful person and have a beautiful home.

I asked God to help us, and I asked my husband to acknowledge his anger and change. I stayed silent to the outside world, even to my family. I resigned myself to a life of pain with my "I'll do it myself" attitude. I continued fervently praying for my husband and myself to change our hurtful ways. The physical injuries continued, but they paled in comparison to the internal injuries I was experiencing. I added injury to injury by remaining silent.

I delved deeper into training myself in the way of confessional theology. I studied and I taught, looking for ways to make my life better. I confessed my sin; I received forgiveness. I was declared forgiven and told to go in peace. I walked out of Confession into an angry, explosive home. I decided I needed to be more loving, more beautiful, and more forgiving. Nothing worked, and I was scared and dying inside, but still unaware of the deep pain and injuries.

The analogy of the vine being tied too tightly to the wire came to life. I was holding myself so closely to the Law to love that I was doing so in an unhealthy way; that energy was no longer flowing freely but rather being constricted. Then my life took a distinctive turn when I began listening to The Vine speak! I moved into the Gospel of John, and Jesus' words "I am the Vine; you are the branches" gave me hope.

Over a fifteen-year period, the intricacies of the grapevine came to life. I was being trained in a new command and a new, living relationship with God. I watched grafting and took to heart my flesh-on-flesh relationship with Christ. I saw the roots of a mature vine and came to realize that I am rooted and grounded in Christ. I saw the sap flow out of the vine and knew God's energy was at work. I watched my father work in the vines and began to trust that God's work was for me.

I watched the vines being trained up. I developed the courage to listen to loving people that God had placed in my life to help train me. I became healthy enough to question the unhealthy parts of my training as a child in my home, in my marriage, and in my church. I also became healthy enough to ask for help. I watched the trained vines grow and produce fruit. God wanted me to live, and I decided that I wanted to live. Receiving new training takes courage. Courage leads to hope. And hope has not disappointed me.

THE BRANCHES SPEAK: YOUR STORY

Your story and mine are different, but we certainly have a lot in common. We are created by God as multifaceted beings. We long for healthy training. We long to grow. We long for health and healing of body and soul, of mind and heart. God created us this way. If one area is out of balance, our whole being will suffer. Growing up, being trained up in Christ, gives us freedom. Being honest and open is part of the journey.

Sharing in safety, knowing how much to share with the right people, is part of being trained in love. Discuss the following questions with your small group. Share only as much as you feel comfortable sharing, recognizing that we can help bear one another's burdens, but we are to give other people the tools to bear their own load. Share more with God in prayer. Share more with your pastor or with a trusted professional.

1. What has The Vine spoken to you in this chapter?
2. What aspects of your being trained up help you see Jesus' training in a clearer light?
3. What aspects of your training create a stumbling block to seeing Christ's call to train you up?
4. What verses stand out to you as you are being trained up in Christ to love?

Chapter Seven

GROWING IN THE VINE

THE VINE SPEAKS: MY FATHER'S VINEYARD

Energy in grapevines flows constantly at a cellular level, bringing continual growth and change. The growth during spring is the most noticeable because it is very rapid green growth bursting forth from dormant vines. Tender shoots from the branches grow as much as two inches on a warm spring day. Shoot growth takes place from April through July when the canes reach the optimum three-foot length.

Shoot Growth

The tender shoot growth is the process of unfolding what is tightly wound up in the bud. A microscopic cross section of the bud before bud break reveals all of the leaf surface and the fruit for the coming season. This year's growth was formed in the bud grown last season. All of this year's growth is intimately connected to previous and future years. Very few plants contain this mystery.

The energy of the vine shifts from rapid shoot growth to fruit maturation in August. The fruit ripens fully and is harvested in September and October. We cannot see growth in the vine, but we know it occurs throughout this season. The growing vine produces the branches and beautiful fruit, which we see with our eyes. Growth we cannot see with our eyes takes place throughout all seasons and throughout the life of the vine.

Mature Fruit

As shoots grow upward in the sunlight, the roots grow down, seeking nutrients and water in the soil. Growth slows in the cool soil of winter and is more rapid in the spring and summer. The roots, which we cannot see, as well as the vine and branches we can see need oxygen in order to grow.

The trellis system provides uniform structure for the plants. Growth takes place within the boundaries of the structure, so there is an element of sameness. However, the vinedresser allows the branches freedom to grow and produce fruit within that structure. The result is beautifully individual vines within the vineyard.

Growing and producing quality fruit is what vines do naturally. If our vines do not grow, my father assesses the problem and takes action. If he cannot figure out how to address the problem, he brings in experts to help identify and attack the problem.

The Vine Speaks: Jesus' Words

I am the true vine, and My Father is the vinedresser. Every branch in Me that does not bear fruit He takes away, and every branch that does bear fruit He prunes, that it may bear more fruit. Already you are clean because of the word that I have spoken to you. Abide in Me, and I in you. As the branch cannot bear fruit by itself, unless it abides in the vine, neither can you, unless you abide in Me. I am the vine; you are the branches. Whoever abides in Me and I in him, he it is that bears much fruit, for apart from Me you can do nothing. (John 15:1–5)

As they journeyed with Jesus, His followers were afforded only one option—growth. Their lives changed instantly when The Vinedresser grafted their lives into The Vine. And growth in Him occurred throughout their lives. At times, they grew rapidly; at other times, growth was slower. Growing is what followers of Christ do. If a branch of The Vine doesn't grow, it means there is a problem that needs to be identified and addressed. In the next chapter, we will take a look at challenges in the vineyard and how they are handled; for now, we'll focus on growing in The Vine.

Jesus' call to follow and the subsequent journey in His holy life provided His followers all they needed to grow. The Vine knew His journey to the cross would not be easy for His disciples. Right in the middle of John's record of that journey, Jesus declared Himself The Vine and them the branches. They had a living, growing, flesh-on-flesh relationship with Him, grafted into His holy life. Energy and life came from Him. They grew because of who The Vine is and what He does naturally.

The Vine speaks growing words in John 15. Perhaps Jesus had spoken "The Vine and the branches" words to His disciples while they were walking through a vineyard. Perhaps, as He talked about creating the vine with so many beautiful parallels to His life and work, He was refreshing their memory. Perhaps this was the first time they heard these words. Imagine the disciples in the Upper Room, clean because of the Word The Vine spoke; confused because of the Word He spoke; comforted because of the Word He spoke. Ponder and discuss the following words in light of the rapid growth in the hearts of the disciples:

- I am the vine; you are the branches. Whoever abides in Me and I in him, he it is that bears much fruit, for apart from Me you can do nothing. (John 15:5)

- If you abide in Me, and My words abide in you, ask whatever you wish, and it will be done for you. (v. 7)

- If you keep My commandments, you will abide in My love, just as I have kept My Father's commandments and abide in

His love. These things I have spoken to you, that My joy may be in you, and that your joy may be full. (vv. 10–11)

- This is My commandment, that you love one another as I have loved you. Greater love has no one than this, that someone lay down his life for his friends. You are My friends if you do what I command you. (vv. 12–14)

John's Spirit-led record of The Vine's words challenges us to grow. We've been correctly taught that Jesus is the divine lover and keeper of the Law, which He kept perfectly in our place. He loved perfectly. He died in our place as the ultimate act of love. These words commanding us to "love and keep" challenge our faith and bring growth. The Vine declares that His call to "love and keep" brings Him joy and brings us joy.

Jesus didn't say "I'll love and keep for you." He said, "If you love Me, keep" and "I've given you an example." And He said so much more! He declared our life in Him and His in us. These are growing-up words. The Vine provides the life and energy we need to grow up in love and keep and do what He commands. Think back to the trellis system onto which the vines are trained (chapter 6). The trellis system (Law) provides structure so the branches in the vine have the support and freedom to do what healthy branches do naturally (grow and bear fruit). From the context of abiding, we love and keep.

The Vine speaks! His interaction with Philip challenges us to grow in several ways. First, Jesus' way and Philip's way were different. Philip told Jesus he wanted to grow by seeing the Father; Jesus said, "Look closely, whoever has seen Me has seen My Father." Second, Jesus calls Philip to trust His word and gave him opportunity to trust by seeing His work. Third, Jesus patiently calls Philip to grow in Him, and in that call, Jesus provided everything Philip needed to grow:

Philip said to Him, "Lord, show us the Father, and it is enough for us." Jesus said to him, "Have I been with you so long, and you still do not know Me, Philip? Whoever has seen Me has seen the Father. How can you say, 'Show us the Father'? Do you not believe that I am in the Father and the Father is in Me? The words that I say to you I do not speak on My own authority, but the Father who dwells in Me does His works. Believe Me that I am in the Father and the Father is in Me, or else believe on account of the works themselves." (John 14:8–11)

In the next verses, The Vine speaks even more challenging words to Philip and the disciples. Every time I read these words, I think about what the disciples thought when Jesus spoke to them, and my wonderment increases. Did Jesus mean these words only for the disciples? Narrowing these words is as dangerous as being puffed up with the pride of bearing fruit. John wrote his Gospel "that [we] may believe that Jesus is the Christ, the Son of God, and that by believing [we] may have life in His name" (John 20:31). These words are a call to grow, and as we grow, we bear fruit because that is what healthy branches of the vine do.

Truly, truly, I say to you, whoever believes in Me will also do the works that I do; and greater works than these will he do, because I am going to the Father. Whatever you ask in My name, this I will do, that the Father may be glorified in the Son. If you ask Me anything in My name, I will do it. (John 14:12–14)

The Vine spoke more "growing-up" words:

- Then they said to Him, "What must we do, to be doing the works of God?" Jesus answered them, "This is the work of God, that you believe in Him whom He has sent." (John 6:28–29)

- This was why the Jews were seeking all the more to kill Him, because not only was He breaking the Sabbath, but He was even calling God His own Father, making Himself equal with God.

  So Jesus said to them, "Truly, truly, I say to you, the Son can do nothing of His own accord, but only what He sees the Father doing. For whatever the Father does, that the Son does likewise. For the Father loves the Son and shows Him all that He Himself is doing. And greater works than these will He show Him, so that you may marvel. For as the Father raises the dead and gives them life, so also the Son gives life to whom He will." (John 5:16–21)

- When the Spirit of truth comes, He will guide you into all the truth, for He will not speak on His own authority, but whatever He hears He will speak, and He will declare to you the things that are to come. He will glorify Me, for He will take what is Mine and declare it to you. All that the Father has is Mine; therefore I said that He will take what is Mine and declare it to you. (John 16:13–15)

Jesus never said, "Wow, look at you, you've grown enough! You've arrived." Even when Jesus rested with the disciples, He taught them an important aspect of growing—restoring. This next interaction between Jesus and His disciples—a call for growth—must be investigated in light of Jesus' words in John 13–15.

His disciples said, "Ah, now You are speaking plainly and not using figurative speech! Now we know that You know all things and do not need anyone to question You; this is why we believe that You came from God." Jesus answered them, "Do you now believe? Behold, the hour is coming, indeed it has come, when you will be scattered, each to his own home, and will leave Me alone. Yet I am not alone, for the Father is with Me. I have said these things to you, that in Me you may have peace. In the world you will have tribulation. But take heart; I have overcome the world." (John 16:29–33)

Jesus may have said, "Growing is hard, but it is necessary to keep growing for your entire life." The Vine spoke these words of comfort: "Take heart; I have overcome the world." Every life Jesus touched He called to grow. Raising the dead was a call to grow. Every storm He calmed was a call to grow. Every person healed was called to grow. Every word He spoke was a call to grow in Him.

Grapevines and branches need soil, oxygen, sunlight, nutrition, and water. Roots need these things as well. We, the branches of The Vine, are grafted into the holy roots of The Vine, which provide stability and draw in nutrients and water. The Vine is the light; The Vine is the living water. His energy, His blood, flows through us, cleansing us from all impurities on a cellular level and giving us what we need to grow in faith in Him.

Growing is what we do. Healthy branches love and keep His commands because He is The Vine and we are grafted into His holy life. Apart from Him, we can do nothing. We cannot grow or produce fruit on our own. The process of growth is not an "only one way for all" package. Growth in The Vine cannot be defined according to neat and tidy standards; our growth is messy because it is an exercise of the heart.

Living branches grow; dead branches don't. Jesus said, "Apart from Me, you can do nothing." We spend an inordinate amount of time talking about and listening for words relating to dying and deadness. Once-dead ears listen and hear *those* words far more readily than words of growing, mercy, and healing. We're quick to think that *alive* and *life* and growing words are for others, not for us.

We were dead in our sin; we are alive in The Vine, and He is alive in us! We need to be trained to listen deeply to growing words and allow them to work in us at a cellular level, just as sap and blood work. The Vine speaks words of life and growth, even when our bodies are fading away. The incredible paradox of our faith and growth is that dying in Christ is a continuation of life in Christ. We are alive, grafted into Christ's life, whether here on earth or face-to-face with Him in heaven. The Vine cries "Ephphatha!"—that is, "Be open!"—into our ears and our hearts and our mouths. Reflect on Mark's account of Jesus' word and work:

> They brought to Him a man who was deaf and had a speech impediment, and they begged Him to lay His hands on him. And taking him aside from the crowd privately, He put His fingers into his ears, and after spitting touched his tongue. And looking up to heaven, He sighed and said to him, "Ephphatha," that is, "Be opened." And his ears were opened, his tongue was released, and he spoke plainly. And Jesus charged them to tell no one. But the more He charged them, the more zealously they proclaimed it. And they were astonished beyond measure, saying, "He has done all things well. He even makes the deaf hear and the mute speak." (Mark 7:32–37)

Jesus' work to bring growth is as untidy and messy as the vinedresser and workers' work in our vineyards. The work is unique to individual branches. The work creates wounds and brings health and growth and balance to the branches of the vine. We want our growth to be sterile and self-controlled and self-contained. The Vine and The Vinedresser don't work that way, and the growth they nurture doesn't either. May our cry be "He has done all things well—messy, but well—for us and in us!"

THE BRANCHES SPEAK: THE APOSTLES' WORDS

The apostles followed Jesus' call and grew up in Christ. The fruit of their growth is before us now in their words and work. They had eyes to see, ears to hear, and hearts and souls that were susceptible to God's work in them. As healthy branches in The Vine, they received, heard, and grew up in Christ. Having grown up, they speak.

The apostle Paul speaks growing words in his letters to the Christians under his care. He nurtures, waters, and brings light and nutrients by speaking Christ. As people received God's Word through him, they grew in love and faith and beautiful actions and knowledge. Paul chastised people if they weren't growing because growth is the only option for branches of The Vine. Paul's energy and passion for Christ's word and work welled up within him so powerfully that he explodes with desire for us to grow:

- For through [Jesus] we both have access in one Spirit to the Father. So then you are no longer strangers and aliens, but you are fellow citizens with the saints and members of the household of God, built on the foundation of the apostles and prophets, Christ Jesus Himself being the cornerstone, in whom the whole structure, being joined together, grows into a holy temple in the Lord. In Him you also are being built together into a dwelling place for God by the Spirit. (Ephesians 2:18–22)

- For this reason I bow my knees before the Father, from whom every family in heaven and on earth is named, that according to the riches of His glory He may grant you to be strengthened with power through His Spirit in your inner being, so that Christ may dwell in your hearts through faith—that you, being rooted and grounded in love, may have strength to comprehend with all the saints what is the breadth and length and height and depth, and to know the love of Christ that surpasses knowledge, that you may be filled with all the fullness of God. (Ephesians 3:14–19)

- Rather, speaking the truth in love, we are to grow up in every way into Him who is the head, into Christ, from whom the whole body, joined and held together by every joint with which it is equipped, when each part is working properly, makes the body grow so that it builds itself up in love. (Ephesians 4:15–16)

- I planted, Apollos watered, but God gave the growth. So neither he who plants nor he who waters is anything, but only God who gives the growth. He who plants and he who waters are one, and each will receive his wages according to his labor. For we are God's fellow workers. You are God's field, God's building. (1 Corinthians 3:6–9)

It is easy for branches of The Vine to get puffed up and assess the growth of branches around them. But judging the growth of others is not within the realm of the branches. Paul offered the Word of God, but God caused growth. Christians who lived in judgment of fellow branches in The Vine were harshly chastised for misusing the gifts with which they had been blessed. He urged them to "grow up."

God's Word through His apostles calls us to trust the hand of the Vinedresser with the understanding that growth is often uncomfortable. God's Word calls us to place ourselves in proximity to that which is needed for growth: living water, the blood of Christ, the Word, and the fellowship of branches. I'm fascinated by this real-life example from the vineyard:

Branches of the grapevine grow tendrils at even intervals. Tendrils wrap around the wire trellis system, creating a spring-like effect to give stability to the vine. My father examined a dying vine closely, only to find that a tendril had wrapped around the trunk of the vine. The tendril had been supple the year it grew around the trunk, but it dried and hardened unnoticed. The trunk tried to grow, but the tendril girdled the trunk, cutting off all sap flow. The branch of this vine choked itself to death.

Paul called branches to grow. He called them to trust God's word and work, to fellowship with growing people, to drink richly of the living water. When we take growth halfheartedly or run from it or even deny it, we may be choking our own life from the life of The Vine.

Growing up in The Vine is not initiated or sustained from within. It is the work of God at work in us. We receive it and submit to it. Paul knew this and proclaimed the power of God (using the word from which we get the word *dynamite*), which raised Jesus from the dead, at work in us (Ephesians 1). In Galatians, Paul makes it clear that the fruit of the Spirit produced in us and through us is the work of God in us and through us.

The New Testament provides many examples of Peter growing up in The Vine. Peter was an exuberant, passionate follower. Imagine the rapid growth that took place in Peter in just these few examples:

- *Jesus washes the disciples' feet—*

  He came to Simon Peter, who said to Him, "Lord, do You wash my feet?" Jesus answered him, "What I am doing you do not understand now, but afterward you will understand." Peter said to Him, "You shall never wash my feet." Jesus answered him, "If I do not wash you, you have no share with Me." Simon Peter said to Him, "Lord, not my feet only but also my hands and my head!" Jesus said to him, "The one who has bathed does not need to wash, except for his feet, but is completely clean. And you are clean, but not every one of you." (John 13:6–10)

- *Peter goes to battle for Jesus—*

Then Simon Peter, having a sword, drew it and struck the high priest's servant and cut off his right ear. (The servant's name was Malchus.) So Jesus said to Peter, "Put your sword into its sheath; shall I not drink the cup that the Father has given Me?" (John 18:10–11)

- *Peter denies Jesus and feels the anguish of that denial—*

And a little later someone else saw him and said, "You also are one of them." But Peter said, "Man, I am not." And after an interval of about an hour still another insisted, saying, "Certainly this man also was with Him, for he too is a Galilean." But Peter said, "Man, I do not know what you are talking about." And immediately, while he was still speaking, the rooster crowed. And the Lord turned and looked at Peter. And Peter remembered the saying of the Lord, how He had said to him, "Before the rooster crows today, you will deny Me three times." And he went out and wept bitterly. (Luke 22:58–62)

In light of these and many other experiences of growing up in The Vine, Peter proclaims these profound words:

Humble yourselves, therefore, under the mighty hand of God so that at the proper time He may exalt you, casting all your anxieties on Him, because He cares for you. Be sober-minded; be watchful. Your adversary the devil prowls around like a roaring lion, seeking someone to devour. Resist him, firm in your faith, knowing that the same kinds of suffering are being experienced by your brother-hood throughout the world. And after you have suffered a little while, the God of all grace, who has called you to His eternal glory in Christ, will Himself restore, confirm, strengthen, and establish you. (1 Peter 5:6–10)

THE BRANCHES SPEAK: MY STORY

Growth means change. There have been times when I embraced growth and change and times when I fought back. When I fought spiritual growth and change, I fought what God designed and desired for me when He grafted me into The Vine. I'm learning that the call to life in The Vine is a call to continued growing every day until the day I meet Jesus face-to-face.

If our vines aren't growing, serious problems exist. If a newborn baby doesn't grow, it's because there are serious problems. If a toddler doesn't grow, serious problems exist. You get the point! Growing and maturing physically is only one aspect of our God-created, very complex beings. Growing and maturing emotionally, mentally, and academically are other aspects of our being.

Growing spiritually is one aspect of Christian life. Learning to trust the hand of The Vinedresser is a major part of spiritual growth. All forms of growth are intimately connected by our Creator's design and are vitally important to life in Him. Balance in all areas of life is critical to growing as human beings and critical to growing in Christ. Growing in one area but not in others creates imbalance and can be very unhealthy. Now, I continue to grow and am learning to embrace all aspects of growth, even though it can be scary.

For a while, though, my life was not balanced, so my growth was not balanced, and I was not healthy. My life was not, *could not* have been balanced because the most significant human relationship in my life generated fear. I had not identified my fear because I was so busy paying attention to my academic growth. I had not recognized my emotional need for security and peace in my home. My life and home had narrowed to my husband and me and my books. My heart cried out for more. At church and in the community, we acted one way, but at home we behaved differently. And that is what it was: a very private act, as I tried to mitigate the anger and balance the pain both of us were living in.

I raced around, trying to make sure angry explosions didn't happen. I constantly attempted to achieve the perfect meal and a well-kept home. I hid my pain from family and friends. I lived with the deep fear that something was really wrong with me. Basic fear led to belief that since my husband was nice to others, I must certainly be the problem. I confessed my sins to God, tried to change my behavior to relieve the angry outbursts, and tried to make myself perfect in every way. No one could see my pain because of my beautiful public performance.

In the vineyard that day, as I watched the sap flow from the wound made by pruning and the process of healing, I prayed that God would bring peace into my home. I had every hope that my husband would change, but I had taken responsibility for making that happen. I was sure my husband would change if only I were better. I was sure that God would work a miracle. Change was necessary, but it could only take place through growing into an understanding of the depth of the pain he was in. I got in the way of growth.

God was calling me to grow and trust His work. I fought His call. I watched the vine grow and visualized Christ's energy and lifeblood working in me. The breakdown of my marriage took place over many years, and that was hard to acknowledge. But I recognized real danger when I finally admitted that I didn't want to be alive anymore. I finally took the courage to recognize that God was calling me to live.

Growing involved feeling pain, something I wasn't accustomed to. Acknowledging the lie I'd lived was painful. Pain has also been caused by others who reject me for the choices I've made. I have been told that I don't value marriage and that I need better communication skills. I have been told I don't trust God. I have been told that loving and valuing myself is not what God's Word calls me to do. I have been told I didn't try hard enough. Other people wanted me to grow according to their own design, and with good intentions, they tried to cause growth.

I kept myself from growing in The Vine in another profound way: lack of growth was caused by self-condemnation. I was getting in The Vine-dresser's way. He forgave me, freely and fully; He tended to my life as a loving Father, and I resisted His work in order to do it myself. I worked so hard on my own, but I was working against the Lord's work and His call to grow.

Growing up in The Vine included identifying areas in which my unhealthy thoughts about myself prevented my growth. I correctly believed that I wasn't worthy of God's grace, and I received His mercy. However, that led me to believe I wasn't worth anything and didn't deserve safety and love. I thought that staying in an unhealthy home was my only option. I also faced the pain of identifying the unhealthy belief that if people really knew me, they wouldn't love me. I'm beginning to comprehend that in a very real, transparent way, knowing one another gives us opportunity to love deeply. I'm learning to trust, and I'm learning to identify trustworthy people.

Every day, I call on God's mercy to help me grow up in The Vine through grieving my losses. As I have grown, I have learned that it takes a tremendous amount of energy to work against God's will and design to grow. Growing comes naturally to branches in a vine. I have learned courage and hope in Christ alone. I am growing to understand the profound nature of His energy at work in me.

Today I embrace the process of growing. Today, when I fall into my old habit of thinking that "I'll do it myself," I recognize it, step back a little more quickly, and ask for help. I have trusted friends who journey this broken road with me. I meet regularly with a trusted Christian mental health care professional. I've grown to appreciate this parallel: an aspect of the healing process when I suffered injury to my body was physical therapy; an aspect of the healing process as I'm growing through the injuries to my heart and spirit is mental therapy. Another aspect of the healing process is immersing myself in the life of The Vine so I may continue to grow up in Him.

Growing up

THE BRANCHES SPEAK: YOUR STORY

Our stories of growing up in The Vine are different because we are different. We are the same, however, in our deep desire to grow and in the fears of growing that we face. We are stubborn and want to do things our way. But The Vine's way is more fruitful and brings us great joy when we follow His call to trust and grow.

Please ponder these questions privately, and then share only what you're comfortable sharing with your group. Your story includes The Vine's work to call you deeper into His life. Please find the courage and find your voice as you speak your story.

1. What has The Vine spoken to you about growing up through this chapter?
2. Identify the verses that have been most meaningful for your growth.
3. Why does growing up in The Vine cause fear, and how does fear restrict growth?
4. Honesty and transparency lead to an authentic life in The Vine. Why is embracing growing up in this way scary?

Chapter Eight

THINNING THE BRANCHES

THE VINE SPEAKS: MY FATHER'S VINEYARD

Thinning is the important annual process of removing healthy but unnecessary shoots and fruit from the cordon. We thin to clean excess growth that would impede sunlight and wind flow. We thin so the energy of the vine is directed to balanced, necessary growth, not consumed by excess growth. We also thin to remove unnecessary growth so the spurs on the cordon are clean for next year's pruning.

Thinning branches of a healthy grapevine takes place from the middle of May through the middle of June, in the late spring after the danger of frost is past. The vines grow rapidly during these months. Thinning fruit takes place, if necessary, during July and August. Thinning and pruning are related in purpose, but vastly different in practice. The purpose of both pruning and thinning is to remove excess to clean and position. During the pruning season, the vines are hardened off, resting for the winter season, and the cut is drastic and is made with a sharp pruning shear.

Little branches that grow during this phase of the season are called shoots. Shoot thinning requires only the gentle pinch of the fingertips,

Before Thinning   After Thinning

which is enough to remove the supple, rapidly growing shoots from the cordon. The primary shoot from each carefully pruned bud grows three to four feet in length and produces two clusters of primary fruit. Recall our discussion of the buds on the vine in chapter 1. Each pruned spur contains two buds that grew last year. These buds grow the shoots that bear fruit this year. Each bud holds within it all of this year's growth, tightly wound up. The primary shoot bears fruit and develops buds for the following year.

A secondary shoot grows from the same bud but comes out about two weeks later. It grows to half the length and grows one small cluster of fruit, called second crop. From the same bud, a third shoot may grow out a week or two later. The third shoot sustains the vine if the primary and secondary shoots should freeze and die during the frost season. The third shoot doesn't grow fruit. These second and third shoots also grow more

Maturing Fruit

leaf surface than is necessary to ripen the fruit. They draw energy from the plant, creating unnecessary strain on the vine.

My father directs our workers to carefully remove every second and third shoot from each bud. Our workers take off many supple, green, growing shoots containing second crop fruit and shoots that are fruit-less. They are thinned from the vine, dropped to the ground, and become part of the vineyard floor. This thinning shapes, cleans, and positions this year's fruit production and provides us positioned and clean spurs for the following year. All of the growth we take off is healthy because the vine is healthy, but it is unnecessary. The growth needs to be positioned and cleaned to bear primary fruit.

Fruit thinning is also an important process for the health and balance of the vine. If there is too much fruit, some must be cut off so the vine can carry the load and ripen the rest of the fruit. The fruit we thin off is not bad fruit. But if it is left on the vine, none of the fruit would mature, and the vine would suffer both this year and in the years to come.

My father assesses the overall balance and health of the vine. If the vine is balanced, we don't thin the fruit. If the vine is carrying too much fruit, we thin some of the fruit and throw it on the ground. The excess fruit, like the pruned canes and thinned shoots, becomes part of the vine-yard floor and provides nutrition for the plants.

THE VINE SPEAKS: JESUS' WORDS

I am the true vine, and My Father is the vinedresser. Every branch in Me that does not bear fruit He takes away, and every branch that does bear fruit He prunes, that it may bear more fruit. Already you are clean because of the word that I have spoken to you. Abide in Me, and I in you. As the branch cannot bear fruit by itself, unless it abides in the vine, neither can you, unless you abide in Me. I am the vine; you are the branches. Whoever abides in Me and I in him, he it is that bears much fruit, for apart from Me you can do nothing. If anyone does not abide in Me he is thrown away like a branch and withers; and the branches are gathered, thrown into the fire, and burned. (John 15:1–6)

Shoot thinning and fruit thinning are important aspects of The Vinedresser's work in our lives. Jesus' words always call an individual or community of individuals to grow and bear fruit, but the growth is to be groomed and the fruit concentrated as the prime fruit. Bearing prime fruit is the end goal. The process of thinning focuses growth and maturing as branches in The Vine. As discerning members of His Body, with a desire to do His work, we follow His call.

Following The Vinedresser means learning to trust His work and His intimate touch in our lives. The Vinedresser takes away every branch in The Vine that does not bear fruit. In the previous chapter, I likened pruning to the heavy, drastic work Jesus did in the hearts of the disciples, preparing them for His death on the cross and their future work of bearing fruit. Here, I liken the process of thinning to Jesus' work in the hearts of His followers who were growing rapidly. He worked this work to focus their growth so they would bear prime fruit.

Jesus called the disciples to fruitful lives, which meant directing energy and attention to where they were called to be fruitful. Simon (Peter), Andrew, James, and John were fishermen. Fishing was their profession, their life's vocation. They worked with their hands and minds to provide food for their families and their community. Jesus sought them where they were fishing, which is also where He met them after His resurrection. Matthew records:

> While walking by the Sea of Galilee, He saw two broth-
> ers, Simon (who is called Peter) and Andrew his brother,
> casting a net into the sea, for they were fishermen. And He
> said to them, "Follow Me, and I will make you fishers of
> men." Immediately they left their nets and followed Him.
> And going on from there He saw two other brothers, James
> the son of Zebedee and John his brother, in the boat with
> Zebedee their father, mending their nets, and He called
> them. Immediately they left the boat and their father and
> followed Him. (Matthew 4:18–22)

Jesus called these men out of their vocation to do His work, using language common to their work. They were fishermen; He called them to be
fishers of men. They were living fruitful lives when Jesus called them. We
don't know many details about them, but we can surmise that their per-
sonalities and passion didn't change with Jesus' call. His work thinned their
lives and focused their energy on the prime fruit He called them to bear.

For this portion of our study, think of The Vine as the trunk as well as
the cordon on the wire. Think of the branches, the disciples, as the shoots
growing out of the buds. Jesus sent them out to bear fruit. When they
returned, He called them to bear the important fruit of resting and eating,
that is, taking care of their physical and emotional needs: "The apostles
returned to Jesus and told Him all that they had done and taught. And
He said to them, 'Come away by yourselves to a desolate place and rest a
while.' For many were coming and going, and they had no leisure even to
eat" (Mark 6:30–31).

Jesus' work and word cleaned and positioned His followers to bear the
prime fruit to which He called them. These examples reflect His work to
thin and focus their lives. These individuals were branches in Him, doing
good works, but He thinned them so the energy of their lives focused on
the prime fruit He desired them to bear.

- The man from whom the demons had gone begged that he might be with Him, but Jesus sent him away, saying, "Return to your home, and declare how much God has done for you." And he went away, proclaiming throughout the whole city how much Jesus had done for him. (Luke 8:38–39)

- Now as they went on their way, Jesus entered a village. And a woman named Martha welcomed Him into her house. And she had a sister called Mary, who sat at the Lord's feet and listened to His teaching. But Martha was distracted with much serving. And she went up to Him and said, "Lord, do You not care that my sister has left me to serve alone? Tell her then to help me." But the Lord answered her, "Martha, Martha, you are anxious and troubled about many things, but one thing is necessary. Mary has chosen the good portion, which will not be taken away from her." (Luke 10:38–42)

- Then Simon Peter, having a sword, drew it and struck the high priest's servant and cut off his right ear. (The servant's name was Malchus.) So Jesus said to Peter, "Put your sword into its sheath; shall I not drink the cup that the Father has given Me?" (John 18:10–11)

- [Jesus] called the twelve together and gave them power and authority over all demons and to cure diseases, and He sent them out to proclaim the kingdom of God and to heal. And He said to them, "Take nothing for your journey, no staff, nor bag, nor bread, nor money; and do not have two tunics. And whatever house you enter, stay there, and from there depart. And wherever they do not receive you, when you leave that town shake off the dust from your feet as a testimony against them." And they departed and went through the villages, preaching the gospel and healing everywhere. (Luke 9:1–6)

In the next example of thinning, Jesus spoke directly to Peter's heart. Peter jumped out of his fishing boat and swam to Jesus. Peter and the disciples ate breakfast with the risen Lord. Jesus' words to Peter cut away all unnecessary fruit.

These thinning words came after Peter had denied Jesus, after Jesus' shocking death, after His miraculous resurrection, and after He appeared to the disciples, who were hiding in isolation and fear. Peter, the fisherman, received a second call to follow Jesus after he had gone back to fishing. Think about this event in terms of thinning fruit Peter might have borne, so he could bear the fruit Jesus called him to bear. I cannot imagine the agony Peter must have felt at Jesus' call to love and follow:

> When they had finished breakfast, Jesus said to Simon Peter, "Simon, son of John, do you love Me more than these?" He said to Him, "Yes, Lord; You know that I love You." He said to him, "Feed My lambs." He said to him a second time, "Simon, son of John, do you love Me?" He said to Him, "Yes, Lord; You know that I love You." He said to him, "Tend My sheep." He said to him the third time, "Simon, son of John, do you love Me?" Peter was grieved because He said to him the third time, "Do you love Me?" and he said to Him, "Lord, You know everything; You know that I love You." Jesus said to him, "Feed My sheep. Truly, truly, I say to you, when you were young, you used to dress yourself and walk wherever you wanted, but when you are old, you will stretch out your hands, and another will dress you and carry you where you do not want to go." (This He said to show by what kind of death he was to glorify God.) And after saying this He said to him, "Follow Me." (John 21:15–19)

Peter was a fisherman! After his master's death, he returned to the life he knew. Jesus' words stung because Peter knew he had promised Jesus he would journey with Him all the way to the cross and yet he denied Jesus three times. Peter's guilt caused him profound grief.

Grief is the process of saying good-bye. Grief is a God-designed aspect of our being, a necessary process of being alive. God calls us to learn to say good-bye to fruit-producing aspects of life that are not the prime fruit we are called to bear. In thinning, we learn to experience love and joy. In grieving, we learn to live love. Peter said good-bye to everything that could have been fruitful in his earthly life, and his life gave way to Jesus' thinning, positioning, and cleaning him to bear prime fruit of a life devoted to Christ's call.

These examples are from the lives of people who were cleaned and positioned by the word Jesus had spoken. They may contain elements of repentance; however, repentance is not the primary message of thinning or pruning. Jesus' call was to thin, to grow, and to focus all energy on Him. Jesus positioned followers to bear primary fruit. Thinning takes away unnecessary shoots and fruit. It is a necessary process for the growing, fruit-bearing branch.

We're called to allow Jesus' words to sink into our hearts and into the fiber of our being in our present place in life. Jesus does not call all people to give up everything and follow Him in full-time ministry in the Church. Jesus does call us to passionately pursue the fruit He calls us to bear from the context of abiding in The Vine, wherever we serve. We draw our strength and energy from His holy life as His life flows in us and through us. Jesus' call to thin focuses our efforts and gives us joy in loving and serving and receiving where we're called.

The Branches Speak: The Apostles' Words

Living in Christ, The Vine, means growing and bearing fruit. Followers of Christ were not given an instruction manual detailing exactly where they were to bear fruit. They wrestled with the thinning process as they discerned God's call and desire for them. The call to follow and to bear fruit included the call to freedom within the call and wisdom to discern. Jesus grafted His followers into His life, trained them up, pruned them to bear more fruit, and thinned the branches that didn't bear fruit.

Paul's letter to the Church of Philippi provides examples of the beauty of bearing fruit from the context of life in Christ. Paul also wrestles with the call to allow The Vinedresser to thin the shoot and fruit so that he bears prime fruit:

- For to me to live is Christ, and to die is gain. If I am to live in the flesh, that means fruitful labor for me. Yet which I shall choose I cannot tell. I am hard pressed between the two. My desire is to depart and be with Christ, for that is far better. But to remain in the flesh is more necessary on your account. Convinced of this, I know that I will remain and continue with you all, for your progress and joy in the faith, so that in me you may have ample cause to glory in Christ Jesus, because of my coming to you again. (Philippians 1:21–26)

- So if there is any encouragement in Christ, any comfort from love, any participation in the Spirit, any affection and sympathy, complete my joy by being of the same mind, having the same love, being in full accord and of one mind. Do nothing from selfish ambition or conceit, but in humility count others more significant than yourselves. Let each of you look not only to his own interests, but also to the interests of others. (Philippians 2:1–4)

We must be careful with these verses as we contemplate shoot thinning and fruit thinning. Caring for ourselves is part of the fruit God calls us to bear. Taking care of ourselves so we can care for others is not selfish. Healthy branches "look not only to [their] own interests, but also to the interests of others." We prove ourselves to be emotionally and spiritually unhealthy if we *only* look out for the interests of others.

In the same chapter of Philippians, Paul speaks some often-avoided words. Paul doesn't say our salvation comes by our obedience; he says salvation is in Christ alone. We are grafted into the life of The Vine. We are positioned in Him to bear fruit; we are made clean. We are called to live life as a holy calling in The Vine; we are called to be in awe at bearing His fruit. God works in us so that we bear primary fruit for His good pleasure and purpose. Wrestle with these words:

> Therefore, my beloved, as you have always obeyed, so now, not only as in my presence but much more in my absence, work out your own salvation with fear and trembling, for it is God who works in you, both to will and to work for His good pleasure. Do all things without grumbling or disputing, that you may be blameless and innocent, children of God without blemish in the midst of a crooked and twisted generation, among whom you shine as lights in the world, holding fast to the word of life, so that in the day of Christ I may be proud that I did not run in vain or labor in vain. (Philippians 2:12–16)

Paul's words to the people of Colossae are especially meaningful as we ponder thinning the branches and fruit of the vine. These words bear fruit for us:

Put on then, as God's chosen ones, holy and beloved, compassionate hearts, kindness, humility, meekness, and patience, bearing with one another and, if one has a complaint against another, forgiving each other; as the Lord has forgiven you, so you also must forgive. And above all these put on love, which binds everything together in perfect harmony. And let the peace of Christ rule in your hearts, to which indeed you were called in one body. And be thankful. Let the word of Christ dwell in you richly, teaching and admonishing one another in all wisdom, singing psalms and hymns and spiritual songs, with thankfulness in your hearts to God. And whatever you do, in word or deed, do everything in the name of the Lord Jesus, giving thanks to God the Father through Him. (Colossians 3:12–17)

Peter's grief turned to joy, which he expressed magnificently in the fruit he bore through his letters. Peter calls us to love one another with a pure heart. He says that the One who has called us is holy, so we should be holy in His life. He declared, "You are a chosen race, a royal priesthood, a holy nation, a people for His own possession, that you may proclaim the excellencies of Him who called you out of darkness into His marvelous light. Once you were not a people, but now you are God's people; once you had not received mercy, but now you have received mercy" (1 Peter 2:9–10). From that context, we submit to The Vinedresser's hand, thinning our lives so that we bear prime fruit in Him.

Growing and bearing primary fruit, according to our positioning and calling in Christ, is a message of the Scriptures. Christ has set us free to grow and to bear fruit. "Being in Christ" bears fruit, just as "doing in Christ" bears fruit. Think back to chapter 4 and our discussion of the energy of The Vine. Jesus worked the works He saw His Father doing. We watch Jesus work, and we work His work, which includes but is not limited to prayer and reflection, rest and play, growing and maturing, work or retirement, cleaning our homes and cooking meals, raising children or grandchildren, and serving with our hands and heart.

THE BRANCHES SPEAK: MY STORY

I met Betty Jean at a women's retreat in Hawaii. Betty Jean was frail, unkempt, and too weak to attend full sessions. At one of the sessions at the retreat, I spoke about both receiving and giving as part of the thinning process and the prime fruit we bear. Group members talked openly about their attempts at serving Betty Jean. They tried to take food to her home and help her with housework. Their attempts were offensive to her, however, and she rejected the help of even her closest friends. She had spent a lifetime giving and serving, but she had never learned to receive.

We discussed the challenges of receiving because receiving means admitting we have needs. Betty Jean was accustomed only to giving. I taught that receiving gracefully was part of God's work to thin our lives and the fruit God calls us to bear. I gently suggested to Betty Jean that she allow The Vinedresser to thin away her giving so the fruit of receiving could be brought forth. This would bring balance to her life and fulfill her needs. A focus of the fruit in her life would become allowing others to serve her. Saying thank-you gracefully was also part of the fruit she was called to bear.

The next time I was in Hawaii to lead a retreat, I didn't recognize the spry, eighty-year-old Betty Jean who embraced me with a strong hug. She told me that she had never thought about how receiving care was fruitful. Then she learned and believed and practiced that in receiving, we give others a beautiful opportunity to serve us as Christ's hands and heart in this world. She articulated that as soon as she allowed others the opportunity to serve her, she got stronger. She also said that God taught her a lot about saying thank-you with a humble heart.

Giving and serving is a blessing, and it isn't bad fruit or wrong; it just may not be our calling at a particular time. As I have grown up in Christ, I have been called to examine my shoot growth and fruit bearing. I can get a lot done in any given day, but important questions are: Am I bearing the prime fruit to which God calls me, or am I bearing just a secondary crop or even shoot growth without any fruit? Do I want the hand of The Vinedresser working on the rapidly growing shoots and fruit in my life, positioning me and cleaning me for His purpose?

The grapevines have spoken to me about excess shoot growth and bearing secondary fruit. Excess shoots and fruit don't serve a purpose in our vineyard. Thinning causes a small wound on the vine, which heals quickly. Additionally, the thinned shoots and fruit become part of the soil, bringing nutrients and richness to the growing plant. It hurts to say "I'm not going to bear fruit here or there." It takes courage to say "I'm going to focus on bearing this primary fruit to which God is calling me." It takes maturity to say "I have limitations, and as important as other work is, I cannot say yes."

Learning to say no is an important process of growing in The Vine, perhaps more important than learning to say yes in some cases. Asking for wisdom and discernment has been part of my process of maturing in The Vine. Watching my father work as the vinedresser has also helped me learn that receiving the decisions of The Vinedresser goes against my "I'll do it myself" mentality. We don't do this ourselves. Jesus said, "The Vinedresser takes away every branch in Me that does not bear fruit."

When my children were small, I was very busy as a part-time director of Christian education, seventh- and eighth-grade teacher, and day-care director. As I flew through the braille room with my children in tow, a woman asked, "Cindy, when do you have time to clean your house?" Thinking I was funny, I said, "Let's just put it this way; you're not invited over right now." I've thought about her words and mine many times in light of bearing fruit. I was so busy bearing fruit at church that I didn't have time to bear the fruit of keeping my home clean.

God worked to thin out the places where I was bearing secondary fruit because I needed more time to bear primary fruit in my own home. When I was too busy, everything I accomplished was secondary fruit. None of the fruit I was bearing was wrong or bad, but none of it was concentrated, primary fruit. Additionally, I wasn't bearing the important fruit of receiving or resting, and I certainly wasn't growing up in The Vine.

As God continued to work *in* me so He could work *through* me, He made me aware of some of my fruit-bearing process. After I retired from professional church work, I worked in the vineyard. I realized that when I was driving a tractor, I felt like I needed to be teaching; when I was teaching, I felt like I needed to be driving a tractor. I learned to ask the hard question, "Does my doing define my being, or does my being define my doing?" From that context, I have grown at the hand of The Vinedresser as He cleans up and positions me to bear fruit. Asking myself that question before saying yes or no to any call to bear fruit has brought greater fulfillment in my journey.

The Vinedresser has also made me aware that a lot of my fruit bearing was a cry to have my own emotional needs met. I taught Bible studies with a joy-filled heart and a deep desire to speak as I have been spoken to, but there was a nagging, deeper need. I needed to be taught, and I needed to receive the Word of God from mature Christians.

As I sought to reach out and help other families, I did so with the most beautiful intentions, but also with the underlying hope that someone would help me. I bore a lot of fruit, but it could be only secondary fruit because I had not paid attention to my own need for growth and healing. It was scary, and I felt quite selfish as God was calling me to say "I need to focus on the primary fruit God is calling me to bear—receiving help and learning to say thank-you."

As I thought about the nutrient-rich soil made richer by the cuttings from pruning or shoot thinning, I began to comprehend Paul's words: "Rejoice always, pray without ceasing, give thanks in all circumstances; for this is the will of God in Christ Jesus for you. Do not quench the Spirit" (1 Thessalonians 5:16–19). Paul's words call us to give thanks *in* all circumstances, not *for* all circumstances. Paul calls us to allow the Spirit of God to work freely in our lives to cause growth.

My fears had kept me staunchly attached to the teaching I had received and ensconced in my incorrect interpretation that God worked only through repentance and forgiveness. Still, The Vine spoke to me, saying, "Allow Me to thin the excess shoots and fruit. Grow, grow, grow and bear fruit differently according to My work at work in you. Eventually I'll work *through* you, but for this season I'm working *in* you. My work cannot be put into a neat and tidy box—not for you, not for anyone. I know you're scared, but I am with you; I promise."

While repentance and forgiveness certainly play a role, I couldn't bear primary fruit until I woke up to the physical and emotional pain I was ignoring in the context of my unhealthy home. The Vinedresser thinned out excess shoot growth and fruit. The Vinedresser brought me to the prime fruit of allowing Him to work in me. From that context, I was able to acknowledge that I was spending my energy trying to achieve growth and fruit on someone else's branches.

Learning to say yes and learning to say no are important aspects of God thinning our lives, positioning us to bear primary fruit. Growing into authenticity and openness, learning to say "thank-you" and "please help" are also God's work to thin and position us to bear primary fruit in Him. Thinning branches and fruit opens the canopy to allow airflow and sunlight. Thinning in our lives opens us to much-needed oxygen and sunlight in our lives.

THE BRANCHES SPEAK: YOUR STORY

We can and do and could bear fruit in many places in many ways. We are confidently positioned in Christ's holy life to bear fruit. We wrestle in holy awe with where God calls us to bear fruit. Jesus calls us to ask God for wisdom and discernment; Jesus calls us to meditate on our position in Him to bear fruit; Jesus calls us to rest and to receive, to give and to do.

Thinning takes place during rapid growth, whereas pruning is more drastic and takes place during a dormant season. When we grow rapidly, we want to grow shoots rapidly, to bear fruit everywhere, even if it is secondary fruit or shoots with no fruit. Discuss the following with your small group, and discuss further with God and a trusted mentor.

1. What has The Vine spoken to you in this chapter on thinning the branches and fruit?
2. What is God calling you to thin away so your growth and fruit are more focused and positioned for coming years?
3. Grief is the important process of saying good-bye. How do the examples given above help you discern areas of your life where you need to say good-bye?
4. Who can you reach out to for wisdom and help for discernment in God's will for the fruit you bear?

Chapter Nine

Pruning the Branches

The Vine Speaks: My Father's Vineyard

Pruning is the annual process of cutting away almost all of the previous year's growth. It is a drastic project that positions the spurs on the cordon for optimum fruit production and cleans up unnecessary wood. Pruning the fruit-bearing branches is critical to the balance and health of the vine and to the quality of fruit for both the current year and the next. Cutting away branches that could bear secondary fruit positions the remaining branches to bear the prime fruit.

Every single bud on every branch has the potential to bear fruit. But the result of an unpruned branch is an overabundance of very poor quality fruit that will not ripen properly. The fruit is not bad; it's just not the prime fruit the vine can bear. The clusters of fruit would be small and would lack intensity, and the energy of the vine cannot bring even ripeness.

Pruning takes place after the harvest when the vines are dormant for the winter (December to March). The sap flow has slowed with the onset of frost and cold weather. The wood of the branches is hardened with a thin bark that has formed during the growing season. The leaves have fallen off.

Dormant Vines

My father, the vinedresser, assesses the vines in each vineyard block differently. He makes the necessary cuts with large pruning shears, explaining his plan to our work force as he goes. Workers refer to his example as they prune individual fields. Different types of training systems require different types of pruning, so my father oversees the process in every field.

One type of trellis system in our vineyard is the bilateral cordon system. The cordon spans three feet on each side of the trunk and remains from year to year, tied to the trellis structure. Dad chooses eight to ten well-positioned primary spurs per side to leave on the cordon. He cuts off every branch that is not evenly spaced or isn't a chosen spur (the width of his hand is his measuring tool). The cordon is cleaned of excess wood and extra buds by pruning them, cutting them off at the cordon. Dad begins work on the primary spur, making sure his precise cut leaves only two buds on the primary canes on the cordon. The rest of the previous year's growth is pruned away, leaving eight to ten spurs with two buds per spur.

The tangled branches that are pruned are placed on the ground and chopped into small pieces. These branches become part of the vineyard floor, a natural mulch that is rich in nutrients unique to and necessary for vines. Over the years, the mulch breaks down and becomes part of the soil, creating a fertile environment and a well-balanced home for beneficial insects.

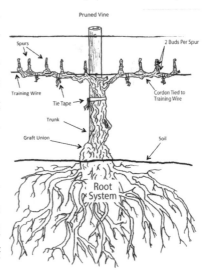

Vine balance and quality fruit production is the goal of pruning. Health and longevity of the vine is achieved by growing the proper amount of

Pruning

branches and fruit production on each vine. If too many spurs are left on the cordon, all of the spurs become weaker. If too much fruit is grown, the vines weaken.

Every year in the life of the vine is intricately connected to past and future years. Last year's canes produced this year's buds, and next year's buds grow in this year's wood. If left unpruned, the vines would literally grow into a jungle of branches and leaves and fruit. Unpruned vines bear fruit, but not prime fruit. Growth for next year's crop would not be positioned properly if the vines were not pruned. A pruned vineyard is a beautiful sight as it is prepared and resting, ready to burst forth with growth in the spring.

There is no bad fruit on a healthy grapevine, but if the buds on the branches are not pruned, there will be too much fruit. The overabundance of fruit diminishes the quality of the clusters. Ten spurs per cordon, two shoots per spur, two clusters per shoot is our particular practice. Other vineyards may have different practices, but all prime vineyards prune annually.

THE VINE SPEAKS: JESUS' WORDS

I am the true vine, and My Father is the vinedresser. Every branch in Me that does not bear fruit He takes away, and every branch that does bear fruit He prunes, that it may bear more fruit. Already you are clean because of the word that I have spoken to you. Abide in Me, and I in you. As the branch cannot bear fruit by itself, unless it abides in the vine, neither can you, unless you abide in Me. I am the vine; you are the branches. Whoever abides in Me and I in him, he it is that bears much fruit, for apart from Me you can do nothing. If anyone does not abide in Me he is thrown away like a branch and withers; and the branches are gathered, thrown into the fire, and burned. (John 15:1–6)

The branches of the vine were grafted into the root of the vine in their first year of life. During their second and third years, the branches of the vine were trained up on the trellis system. After being trained up, vines are pruned annually for the life of the vine. Jesus' words "Every branch that does bear fruit He prunes, that it may bear more fruit" have been quoted often in studies about repentance or discipline. There are elements of repentance and discipline in these words, to be sure, but there is also so much more. Jesus wasn't speaking about anything bad or negative; He says that branches are pruned with the purpose of bearing more fruit.

The Greek word for prune, *kathairō*, means "to cleanse, purify, or position." This word is intimately connected to the word katharos, clean, pure, and clear in a natural sense from the pollution and guilt of sin, without stain or spot. Read Jesus' words again in light of these definitions: "I am the true vine, and My Father is the vinedresser. Every branch in Me that does not bear fruit He takes away, and every branch that does bear fruit He prunes [*kathairō*], that it may bear more fruit. Already you are clean [*katharos*] because of the word that I have spoken to you."

Jesus could have said, "My Father does this work, cleansing and positioning you for fruitful living. Your hearts and minds are going to be really challenged over these next hours as I journey toward the cross and to My death. I'll pass through the grave, but you don't know that yet. Take heart; you are grafted into My life and positioned (pruned) in Me. Faith that My Father's work is being accomplished in Me is part of the fruit you bear through Me because I have declared you clean, without stain or guilt."

Pruning means positioning. Consider also the position of Jesus' words in John 15. Jesus' declaration of Himself as "the vine" positioned Him as The Vine in whom we live and through whom life and energy flow. The context for these words is critical for our study. Jesus spoke these words to keep you from falling away. Ponder the progression of powerful events prior to The Vine speaking the words about pruning:

- In John 11, Jesus declared, "I am the resurrection and the life" (v. 25). Jesus raised His friend Lazarus from the dead by calling him from death to life with His word.

- In John 12, Jesus received a preburial anointing with oil from Mary while her brother Lazarus reclined with Jesus; Jesus entered Jerusalem; Jesus foretold His own death; a voice from heaven called out that Jesus' name had been glorified by His word and work; Jesus declared that whoever has seen Him has seen the Father.

- In John 13, Jesus served the Lord's Supper, washed the disciple's feet, gave a new command to love one another, and foretold Peter's denial.

- In John 14, Jesus declared, "I am the way, and the truth, and the life" (v. 6). He also declared, "Whatever you ask in My name, this I will do" (v. 13); and Jesus promised the Holy Spirit would work in them to bring everything He said to their memory.

Think about the progression of events after Jesus said "I am the vine; you are the branches":

- In John 15, Jesus declared, "If the world hates you, know that it hated Me before it hated you" (v. 18). Jesus also declared, "[The Helper] will bear witness about Me. And you also will bear witness [about Me]" (vv. 26–27).

- In John 16, Jesus declared, "I have said all these things . . . to keep you from falling away" (v. 1), meaning, "to keep you positioned in Me." Jesus declared, "The Spirit of truth [My Spirit] . . . will guide you into all truth . . . [and] whatever He hears He will speak" (v. 13), meaning, "He will speak what He hears from Me." Jesus promised, "Your sorrow will turn to joy" (v. 20), and "Take heart; I have overcome the world" (v. 33).

- In John 17, Jesus prayed a powerful prayer for the disciples and for us, thanking God for what had been accomplished and what is yet to be accomplished.

- In John 18–19, Jesus, the perfect Lamb of God, was arrested, tried, convicted, crucified, and buried.

- In John 20, Jesus rose from the grave.

Pruning was taking place as Jesus positioned the disciples into a deeper relationship with Him. His word and work positioned them to bear the fruit to which He called them; everything else was pruned away. Jesus only was the focus of the drastic cleanup project, positioning the disciples in Him for the purpose of faith and its activity through love. Jesus had grafted them into His life, trained and positioned them to be witnesses of His perfect life, His word, His work, His death, and His resurrection. The Vine has done and is doing the same work for us and in us today.

Pruning is a drastic event. It takes place annually, when there are no green leaves and the vines are resting for the winter. The vines appear dead. The sap flows slowly in the vine and bleeds just enough to form a scab over the wounds made by the pruning shears. I wrestle with the concept of pruning. The pruning the disciples received from The Vinedresser through Jesus' word and work, I believe, took place in the Upper Room. It was a drastic event of cutting away and positioning them. It was scary and hard, but the purpose was a deeper faith and more fruit. Pruning led the disciples to cling to Jesus only and bear only the prime fruit God called them to bear.

The vinedresser prunes the branches so they bear more fruit; the cuttings fall to the soil and become part of the nutrients for the process of bearing prime fruit. The Vinedresser pruned the lives of the disciples. The cuttings fell to the soil of their lives and became part of the nutrients in the growing process of bearing prime fruit in His kingdom. Each disciple was a unique individual with unique life experiences that could have led to fruit in many areas. But The Vinedresser, through the intense cleanup project in the Upper Room, chose what to cut away so their energy was focused on the prime fruit to which He called them. Pruning positioned them to bear more fruit than they would have on their own.

A note on John 15:6 is helpful to distinguish between thinning and pruning branches that are in the vine from throwing away branches that are not. Jesus takes a drastic step regarding the ones who do not "abide in the vine." He said, "If anyone does not abide in Me he is thrown away like a branch and withers; and the branches are gathered, thrown into the fire, and burned" (John 15:6).

When grapevines in our vineyard are diseased, we tear them out and burn them. They cannot be used as mulch like the pruned healthy branches that become part of the soil. John's words in chapter 13 shed light on the difference between being positioned in Christ and not abiding in Christ. John recorded the Passover celebration and Jesus establishing Himself as the new covenant. John recorded that the devil had already put into the heart of Judas Iscariot to betray Jesus.

The devil positioned Judas to do his work. We know that God worked through Judas's evil actions to bring His salvation plan to fruition, but Judas was a branch who didn't remain positioned in The Vine. Judas, by the evil intentions in his heart, was pruned from The Vine. Jesus told him, "Do what you must do and do it quickly." Jesus knew what was going to happen, and He willingly allowed Judas to betray Him:

> Now before the Feast of the Passover, when Jesus knew that His hour had come to depart out of this world to the Father, having loved His own who were in the world, He loved them to the end. During supper, when the devil had already put it into the heart of Judas Iscariot, Simon's son, to betray Him, . . . Jesus . . . rose from supper. . . .
>
> Jesus was troubled in His spirit, and testified, "Truly, truly, I say to you, one of you will betray Me." The disciples looked at one another, uncertain of whom He spoke. One of His disciples, whom Jesus loved, was reclining at table at Jesus' side, so Simon Peter motioned to him to ask Jesus of whom

He was speaking. So that disciple, leaning back against
Jesus, said to Him, "Lord, who is it?" Jesus answered, "It
is he to whom I will give this morsel of bread when I have
dipped it." So when He had dipped the morsel, He gave it
to Judas, the son of Simon Iscariot. Then after he had taken
the morsel, Satan entered into him. (John 13:1–2, 21–27)

Pruning is drastic, and it can be very confusing, as above. Jesus said,
"One of you will betray Me," and the disciples asked, "Lord, who is it?" This
drastic pruning project had the disciples off balance and wondering what
was going on around them. Their hearts wanted to control their position,
but they were being called to submit to the pruning of The Vinedresser.

Another positioning event in the Upper Room took place just before
Judas left, when Jesus washed the disciples' feet. Jesus declared them—but
not *all* of them—"clean," *katharos*, that is, "without spot or blemish." Each
stage of the story reveals just how challenged the disciples were with Jesus'
word and work in their lives. Peter told Jesus no, and when that wasn't the
right answer, he wanted Jesus to wash all of him. Jesus corrected Peter on
both points, declaring that all but one of them were positioned—clean—in
Him. Take note that in the previous example Peter was completely unsure
who was and was not positioned in Christ. John records:

Jesus, knowing that the Father had given all things into
His hands, and that He had come from God and was going back to God, rose from supper. He laid aside His out-
er garments, and taking a towel, tied it around His waist.
Then He poured water into a basin and began to wash the
disciples' feet and to wipe them with the towel that was
wrapped around Him. He came to Simon Peter, who said
to Him, "Lord, do You wash my feet?" Jesus answered him,
"What I am doing you do not understand now, but after-

ward you will understand." Peter said to Him, "You shall never wash my feet." Jesus answered him, "If I do not wash you, you have no share with Me." Simon Peter said to Him, "Lord, not my feet only but also my hands and my head!" Jesus said to him, "The one who has bathed does not need to wash, except for his feet, but is completely clean. And you are clean, but not every one of you." For He knew who was to betray Him; that was why He said, "Not all of you are clean." (John 13:3–11)

Pruning is an intense, drastic cutting away and positioning process during the dormant season, the season the vines are storing up energy for the rapid growth that is coming. Pruning involves cutting and bleeding and healing. Pruning includes allowing buds that cannot produce fruit to fall to the ground to become mulch, providing nutrients for the future. Deep pruning took place in the Upper Room—and as the disciples watched their Lord and Teacher brutally murdered on the cross.

There are elements of repentance in pruning, but repentance is not the main focus. Being positioned to bear more fruit is the main focus. Peter and the disciples were in a constant state of relationship development with Jesus, always in a state of receiving mercy. Jesus' work positioned them and focused everything on His life and work for the life of the world. The pruning they received from The Vinedresser positioned them for lives of bearing the prime fruit He called them to bear.

THE BRANCHES SPEAK: THE APOSTLES' WORDS

The Vine worked in the life of the branches to position them to bear prime fruit. We are beneficiaries of the pruning they received and the "much fruit" they bore as they lived their lives in The Vine. Their experiences at the hand of The Vinedresser through The Vine give us these words to reflect on as we submit our own lives to the hand of The Vinedresser.

Paul was grafted into The Vine by a blinding light, a question from Christ, and the words of Ananias. Paul knew a life of law, hatred, and murder outside of The Vine. Paul, after his conversion, knew life as a man positioned in Christ to bear fruit. The following verses are often used regarding marriage, but Paul intends so much more! These words are about the mystery of Christ and the Church. Examine these verses in light of being pruned as well as all of the other themes we've discussed. Paul helps us understand the relationship between The Vine and the branches:

> Husbands, love your wives, as Christ loved the church and gave Himself up for her, that He might sanctify her, having cleansed [*katharizō* from *kathairō*] her by the washing of water with the word, so that He might present the church to Himself in splendor, without spot or wrinkle or any such thing, that she might be holy and without blemish. In the same way husbands should love their wives as their own bodies. He who loves his wife loves himself. For no one ever hated his own flesh, but nourishes and cherishes it, just as Christ does the church, because we are members of His body. "Therefore a man shall leave his father and mother and hold fast to his wife, and the two shall become one flesh." This mystery is profound, and I am saying that it refers to Christ and the church. However, let each one of you love his wife as himself, and let the wife see that she respects her husband. (Ephesians 5:25–33)

Paul calls us to understand that God works to prune and position us through our callings in life and, in doing so, calls us to a deeper understanding of His work through His Body, the Church. As Paul says, this mystery is profound! We contemplate God's work of creating life and love through the sexual act of husband and wife. Think of the energy involved in creating life. How much more is God's energy at work in creating faith? From that context, we contemplate His creative work in the Church, cleansing through the water and the Word of Baptism as He grafts us into The Vine, trains us up, brings growth, thins and prunes our lives to be fruitful.

Cleansing and positioning is an intimate act, like washing feet or touching a person with leprosy. Being grafted into Christ's Body is a blood-on-blood experience with wounds and scabs and scars. Pruning is also an intimate act of The Vinedresser as He cleanses and positions us in The Vine to bear fruit. Growing and bearing is the goal; God's work positioning us in Christ is one of the many processes toward achieving that goal. As we see, repentance and discipline are aspects of this growth, but they are not the only things.

Abiding *in* The Vine is a position of relationship. John knew the importance of this relationship and reveals more of his thoughts in his letters. Please reflect, first, on Jesus' words and then on John's interpretation of those words:

- [Jesus said,] "I am the true vine, and My Father is the vinedresser. Every branch in Me that does not bear fruit He takes away, and every branch that does bear fruit He prunes, that it may bear more fruit. Already you are clean [positioned] because of the word that I have spoken to you." (John 15:1–3)

- [John said,] "This is the message we have heard from Him and proclaim to you, that God is light, and in Him is no darkness at all. If we say we have fellowship with Him while we walk in darkness, we lie and do not practice the truth.

But if we walk in the light, as He is in the light, we have fellowship with one another, and the blood of Jesus His Son cleanses us from all sin. If we say we have no sin, we deceive ourselves, and the truth is not in us. If we confess our sins, He is faithful and just to forgive us our sins and to cleanse us from all unrighteousness. If we say we have not sinned, we make Him a liar, and His word is not in us." (1 John 1:5–10)

The cleansed life, life in The Vine, is a "walking in the light" life, a transparent life. There is no room for lies or pretending; there is no telling The Vinedresser how He should prune and position us. Being pruned by The Vinedresser was scary and challenging for the disciples. They denied Him, they fled, they cowered, and they argued with one another; they told Jesus what to do and how to do it. He did not submit to them. They submitted to the hand of The Vinedresser.

Peter was perhaps the most challenged by Jesus' word and work, or if not the most challenged, then the most written about. The journey of learning to trust Jesus was hard for the stubborn, self-sufficient fisherman. Time after time, Jesus called Peter to Himself and finally got to Peter's heart after a lot of discussion about loving and feeding sheep (John 21). The promised Holy Spirit settled in on the beautifully positioned Peter and led him to say:

The apostles and the elders were gathered together to consider this matter. And after there had been much debate, Peter stood up and said to them, "Brothers, you know that in the early days God made a choice among you, that by my mouth the Gentiles should hear the word of the gospel and believe. And God, who knows the heart, bore witness to them, by giving them the Holy Spirit just as He did to us, and He made no distinction between us and them, having cleansed [*katharizō*, purified from guilt of sin, positioned] their hearts by faith. (Acts 15:6–9)

Peter's words open our eyes to the understanding of being positioned in The Vine as holy people, cleansed, and purified in an abiding relationship. The purpose of the abiding relationship is that we bear more or much prime fruit. The author of Hebrews was touched by being positioned in the life of The Vine. He makes the connection between Old Testament cleansing to the new covenant as it positions people in Christ:

> For since the law has but a shadow of the good things to come instead of the true form of these realities, it can never, by the same sacrifices that are continually offered every year, make perfect those who draw near. Otherwise, would they not have ceased to be offered, since the worshipers, having once been cleansed, would no longer have any consciousness of sins? But in these sacrifices there is a reminder of sins every year. For it is impossible for the blood of bulls and goats to take away sins.

> Consequently, when Christ came into the world, He said, "Sacrifices and offerings You have not desired, but a body have You prepared for Me; in burnt offerings and sin offerings You have taken no pleasure. Then I said, 'Behold, I have come to do Your will, O God, as it is written of Me in the scroll of the book.'"

> When He said above, "You have neither desired nor taken pleasure in sacrifices and offerings and burnt offerings and sin offerings" (these are offered according to the law), then He added, "Behold, I have come to do Your will." He does away with the first in order to establish the second. And by that will we have been sanctified [cleansed, set apart, made

holy] through the offering of the body of Jesus Christ once for all. (Hebrews 10:1–10)

Jesus calls us to trust His work implicitly, His work only. We are positioned in Him just as my vineyard's 300,000 grapevines are grafted onto rootstock and positioned through pruning to bear fruit. Jesus is The True Vine, and we are grafted into His life, along with all of the saints of all time. By the miracle of life in Him, we are part of one another in the life of The Vine. Being pruned brings challenges. Just like the disciples, then, we are called to trust The Vinedresser now, to submit to the shears, receive the wounds, and allow secondary fruit we might have borne to become part of the soil of our lives. We walk together as Jesus calls us to submit to The Vinedresser's desire to prune our lives for Him.

The Branches Speak: My Story

I've watched pruning up close, and I have pruned vines. The wound the pruning shears make is as drastic as is the amount cut off. Last year's growth, as important as it was to fruit bearing, must go onto the vineyard floor and be chopped up. I've watched and silently wondered, *Wouldn't it be better to leave three buds per spur or more spurs on a cordon? The goal is more fruit, right?* An abundance of quality fruit (the right amount for our vines and trellis system) is the result of achieving that goal.

I've pondered the concept of pruning and its parallel to the Christian life for many years, and I admit that I still wrestle with the concept. Shoot thinning corresponds to The Vinedresser gently plucking away excess growth and secondary fruit. But understanding pruning is hard. I can't wrap my mind around the drastic nature of the pruning I see in the field and any sort of parallel to modern Christian life. We have so much to learn as we bow to God's Word. He positions us to bear the fruit He calls us to bear, to perform, as Paul says, the "good works, which God has prepared beforehand, that we should walk in them" (Ephesians 2:10).

Jesus' call to "follow Me" is drastic. Being grafted into the life of The Vine is the serious process of being cut away from our old self by The Vinedresser and being placed into a new home. Some of us were grafted into Christ's life as infants through Baptism. Some of us were grafted into Christ's life as we came to faith later in life. Being grafted into Christ is a drastic process that changes our dwelling place. Each of us has a story, a journey into God becoming our dwelling place.

Being pruned by The Vinedresser is drastic. I liken it to a journey of learning to trust The Vinedresser's hand as He positions and cleans our lives. Pruning repositions mere knowledge of God to knowing God intimately. Pruning repositions our knowledge from our head to our

heart—which can be a great distance in stubborn, self-sufficient people. Knowing the facts of the Christ in whom we dwell on a cognitive level is necessary and beautiful. Knowing Christ deeply in our heart is Christ's call in our lives. The brain can get in the way of the journey because it is natural to move away from fear, not toward it; it is customary to move away from pain, not submit to it. Jesus calls us to trust Him and love Him with all of our heart and soul and mind.

We get busy thinking that we are practicing trust. We read the Scriptures from an academic perspective, in a comfortable, sterile environment. When Jesus calls us to intimacy, it might include dusty roads and vineyards, mud on blind eyes, and pain and wounds and scars. His promise is that we are in Him and He is in us. He calls us to trust that "by His wounds [we] have been healed" (1 Peter 2:24).

The context of Jesus' "I am the vine" words comes to mind. I can barely begin to imagine the upside-down nature of the lives of the disciples as Jesus turned toward Jerusalem to face the cross. Peter's testimony rings true. He doesn't want Jesus washing his feet, he rebukes Jesus for His words about the cross, and he denies Jesus after vowing that he would go with Him to the cross. Under the circumstances, we would have fled too—and we do flee from fear and dying and death—but the call is to lean into our fears and allow His work to take root and grow.

I needed to spend time—alone time—with The Vinedresser and The Vine and submit to the pruning He had in mind for me. I would not have called it pruning at the beginning of the journey, but today, years later, I am able to draw a parallel. I didn't know how drastic the process would be or that it would be so painful to be a branch in The Vine. The journey started with a simple question from a massage therapist: "Cindy, what hit your head?" My quick reply was "What didn't?" My quip was a mental dash for the door to quickly escape from a very hard question. How could someone ask that by just putting her hand on my head?

I said, "I've been injured a lot," and I recounted a few of the major incidences. She said, "Write about your injuries." Mentally, I bolted for the exit again. I really hadn't written or thought about my injuries and accidents, ever. I was one to quickly move from one event to the next with little thought of process. I was busy bearing beautiful fruit. But in that season of my life, God was starting a drastic pruning project. He stopped me by slowing my energy and placing me in a season of dormancy. He began the process of cleaning and positioning me where and how He wanted me to bear fruit.

The therapist said, "We are human beings, not human doings." That made as much sense as listing my accidents in a journal. After I listed some of the accidents, she commended me and then said, "Now write about your feelings associated with the accidents." Fear gripped me as I thought about the emotions attached to the injuries. I had recorded more than sixty; I couldn't feel. Thinking about how I thought and behaved was difficult. I began writing, and as I wrote, fear tightened its grip. The fear of the process, however, was not greater than the knowledge that what I had been doing wasn't working anymore.

The process of personal discovery prompted a lot of internal questioning. I begged Jesus to lead me to trust in His work and word for me. The vineyard, a place of many accidents, was also the place for unburdening those fears and a place for healing. I watched the wounds of the vines made by the pruning shears heal. I tasted the sap that dripped from the wounds as I meditated on the magnificent healing that the human body is capable of. I reflected on Peter's words "By His wounds you have been healed" (1 Peter 2:24).

Peter's words are past tense: a reality in my life, even in the midst of tremendous personal pain of the journey into my heart and soul. I was scared, and I didn't want to embark on the journey; yet I wanted the journey. A cousin's husband, a pastor, heard a bit of my story and said, "Wow, God is really working in you so He can work through you." I wondered, *Is that what is happening? God working in me so He can work through me? Pruning?* Perhaps.

The apostle John spent an entire chapter telling the story of Jesus healing a man born blind and the subsequent religious struggle with the unorthodox work of God in Jesus. Earth, saliva, and the Word were the means through which Jesus chose to heal. Submitting to mud and spit, the blind man received Jesus at His word! John's Gospel and his exposé of the life of Christ became my dwelling place as I journeyed into a deeper understanding of the Word and work of God for me.

God brought me to a season of dormancy, of resting and personal reflection, to a place of fear and deep questioning. He cut away everything that might have been fruitful so I could bear more fruit, so I could bear His fruit in different ways. I was called to journey into the depth of my pain and sadness and despair, a place where I could cling only to Jesus. I was called to allow Him to cleanse and position me as a branch in The Vine to bear fruit.

I continue to learn to trust with my heart as well as my mind. I'm learning to receive the work of The Vinedresser in my whole being. The Vinedresser's pruning project in my life isn't finished, although the season I described here has passed. I see God's work in my past more clearly. And I know that God's work will continue to position me for the prime fruit He calls me to bear. Pruning wasn't and will never be an academic exercise. Pruning is a call to trust and journey deeper into Jesus' word and work for us and in us and through us.

Learning to Trust

THE BRANCHES SPEAK: YOUR STORY

Your story and mine are different because we are different people, yet we are all created by God as multifaceted beings. God calls us to submit to His hand, and we battle that because we'd rather be in charge. Yet if one area of our life is a tangled mess, we cannot bear abundant fruit. Vine health and balance is our goal, and beautiful, mature fruit is the result of Christ's training and pruning. Being honest and open is part of the journey.

Sharing in safety, knowing how much to share and with whom, is part of the process. Some people try to bear the fruit of helping others when they need to heed their own advice. I speak from firsthand experience! Knowing where we are being asked to bear fruit and maintaining healthy boundaries is an aspect of growing up in Christ.

Discuss the following questions with your small group. Share only as much as you feel comfortable sharing, recognizing that we can help bear one another's burdens, but we are to give other people the tools to bear their own load. Share more with your pastor or with a trusted professional. Share more with God in prayer.

1. What has The Vine spoken to you in this chapter on pruning the vines?

2. How is God at work positioning your life in Him to bear more fruit?

3. What aspects of pruning are you fighting? For example, are you battling fear? severity? Do you feel God isn't working fast enough? Do you think the following? *I like being in control of the process; I'm impatient and want to bear fruit now; I bear too much fruit already!*

4. What verses stand out to you as you are being pruned, positioned, cleaned in Christ to bear fruit?

Chapter Ten

CHALLENGES
AND OPPORTUNITIES

THE VINE SPEAKS: MY FATHER'S VINEYARD

Challenges to the vine and vineyard are present throughout the growing season, and they continue throughout the life of the vines. We have control over some of the challenges we face, so we take action. We don't have control over some of the challenges we face, so we adapt. My father has grown grapevines for fifty years, and he faces new challenges every year. He has learned the art of taking action or adapting as he cares for our vineyard. He has learned patience. He is vigilant as he cares for the vines.

Various challenges we act on include too little or too much water or nutrients, pests, high salt content in soil, and water quality. For example, if we irrigate too much in the spring and early summer, the vines grow too vigorously, creating vegetative flavors in the ripe fruit. If we irrigate too little, the shoots don't grow properly and the fruit doesn't mature properly. By carefully managing the water, we manage the growth of the vines.

Another example of a challenge we can act upon is managing the oxygen flow to the root system. Grapevine roots need oxygen, so we regularly rip and till the soil to provide the best environment for the root system. There are many other challenges we can act on, such as weeds, harmful insects, and animals such as birds, squirrels, deer, and coyotes.

Another challenge we face is matching rootstock and varietal according to our soil and climate. We choose rootstock and the varietal grafted into it a year prior to planting, and the nurseries propagate the varietal and rootstock we choose. Ideally, the match is good and the vine produces prime fruit for thirty years or more. But if not, we can regraft into the healthy rootstock with another varietal to get a better match.

The challenges we adapt to are also plentiful and are primarily related to the weather. Among these are drought, flooding, wind, frost, excessive heat, hail, or rain at the wrong time of the year. For example, frost is welcomed when the vines are dormant, but it is not welcomed after bud break. Rain is coveted during the winter and spring, but not during harvest in the fall. Wind impedes pollination during bloom, but it isn't a problem during the winter dormant season.

My father watches over our vineyard, and he is teaching my son the intricacies of being a master grape grower. He is teaching my son to be aware of the challenges we face. He is also teaching my son that if there is something he doesn't know, he calls in experts for advice on how to address the problems. Together, my father and son act on challenges that can be addressed, and they adapt to what cannot.

Challenges are part of vineyard life. In the midst of extreme challenges, we might not embrace them as opportunities. Later, after much reflection, we talk about those challenges as opportunities to learn and grow.

God is The Vinedresser. He is omnipotent and omniscient. He knows everything about His creation, and He is in control—from the beginning of time as we know it and until the very end of life on this earth as we know it. But the result of the fall is that the branches of The Vine—the people He created for relationship with Him—live with challenges. One of these challenges is misunderstanding God. God, The Vinedresser, has the power to control all things, but He chooses not to. Here is one example: God spoke directly to Adam and Eve as He walked with them in the garden of Eden. Their relationship with Him was perfect, just as He created it to be. God gave only one directive: "Don't eat of the tree of the knowledge of good and evil." Within the directive was the very clear promise of the punishment they would receive if they didn't obey—death (Genesis 2).

We don't understand His command. We wonder why God said "don't" when everything else was perfect freedom. God's command "Don't eat the fruit from this one tree" gave Adam and Eve opportunity for freedom and worship. At Satan's prompting, they mistook God's intentional gift and opportunity. Rather than receiving and worshiping, they chose questioning and doing their own will, which led to blaming and hiding. The result of their disobedience was the punishment God promised.

But our loving God didn't leave Adam and Eve and the rest of sinful mankind to their own devices. He made another promise: the Christ. God promised that in the life of His perfect Son, there would be freedom to receive and to worship and to give with a pure heart. The Vinedresser and His Son, The True Vine, see their work clearly. The branches of The Vine are called to receive the work and the life He offers. The branches of The Vine are called to worship and to freedom in The Vine. The heart of God is filled with joy as people receive His gifts and say thank You.

Another challenge is stubbornness. God gave the people ears to hear and eyes to see, but they rejected His gift and choked themselves off from the life He offered. God told Isaiah; "Go, and say to this people: 'Keep on hearing, but do not understand; keep on seeing, but do not perceive.' Make the heart of this people dull, and their ears heavy, and blind their eyes; lest they see with their eyes, and hear with their ears, and understand with their hearts, and turn and be healed'" (Isaiah 6:9–10).

We are challenged to understand God, making our hearts more dull and our eyes more blind. In His wisdom, God took action so His people would turn from their sin and be healed. The Vinedresser sent prophet after prophet into the midst of the people to call them to life. His work and word always offer healing and growth. He works that work despite the stubborn hearts of the people. The Vinedresser, throughout history, has watched the branches of The Vine receive His mercy, freely give, and worship. The Vinedresser has also watched those who reject His mercy steal and kill and destroy.

God works through challenges. Challenges provide an opportunity to grow. The Old Testament is filled with stories from which we can learn about God working through challenges to give people opportunity to grow and bear fruit. The story of Joseph being thrown into a pit by his brothers provides an example, as extreme challenges turned to opportunity. Joseph reflected on the challenges he faced:

> When Joseph's brothers saw that their father was dead, they said, "It may be that Joseph will hate us and pay us back for all the evil that we did to him." So they sent a message to Joseph, saying, "Your father gave this command before he died: 'Say to Joseph, "Please forgive the transgression of your brothers and their sin, because they did evil to you."' And now, please forgive the transgression of the servants

of the God of your father." Joseph wept when they spoke to him. His brothers also came and fell down before him and said, "Behold, we are your servants." But Joseph said to them, "Do not fear, for am I in the place of God? As for you, you meant evil against me, but God meant it for good, to bring it about that many people should be kept alive, as they are today. So do not fear; I will provide for you and your little ones." Thus he comforted them and spoke kindly to them. (Genesis 50:15–21)

Joseph didn't speak these words as he faced the extreme challenge of being thrown into a pit by his brothers or being sold to nomads. Many years later, however, he claimed the challenges as opportunity for God's work. In the Old Testament, story after story reflects God touching people's hearts, the challenges people faced trusting God's Word, and the growth people experienced when they viewed challenges as opportunities.

THE VINE SPEAKS: JESUS' WORDS

I am the true vine, and My Father is the vinedresser. Every branch in Me that does not bear fruit He takes away, and every branch that does bear fruit He prunes, that it may bear more fruit. Already you are clean because of the word that I have spoken to you. Abide in Me, and I in you. As the branch cannot bear fruit by itself, unless it abides in the vine, neither can you, unless you abide in Me. I am the vine; you are the branches. Whoever abides in Me and I in him, he it is that bears much fruit, for apart from Me you can do nothing. (John 15:1–5)

God manifested Himself to speak to our challenges when He sent His Son into this world. The Vine speaks! Jesus was challenged to speak the Word in a way that touched people's hearts and turned their hearts toward Him. The words of John 15 are relationship words, opportunity words. They are a call to comprehend who Jesus is for us and in us as well as a profound picture of life in Him. His words are an offer, a gift, and an opportunity. Contained within the gift are the energy and power and life to live in Him.

One of the tasks Jesus was to accomplish was touching stubborn branches with His word and work. He continually called them to grow in faith and in their understanding of The Vine. He called them to receive His work in them; He called them to comprehend that abiding and loving and keeping were His work in them; He called them to grow. The Vine-dresser and The Vine do the work; branches receive and abide.

Growing leaves and fruit is the purpose of branches, but they cannot accomplish that work on their own. Apart from The Vine, branches can do nothing. They are intimately connected, grafted into The Vine; in Him, they live and thrive and produce. Jesus' word and work call the branches to that work continually. Jesus called people to trust in Him alone.

Some people trusted Jesus at His word and worshiped Him. Those whom He grafted in He also thinned and pruned, that is, cleansed and positioned. They received Him, they heeded His command to love, and they kept His commands as they bore fruit for Him. Reflect on these examples of people being challenged and taking Jesus' words of opportunity:

- *Jesus and the Samaritan woman shared this interaction—*
  The woman said to Him, "I know that Messiah is coming (He who is called Christ). When He comes, He will tell us all things." Jesus said to her, "I who speak to you am He." . . . Many Samaritans from that town believed in Him because of the woman's testimony, "He told me all that I ever

did." So when the Samaritans came to Him, they asked Him to stay with them, and He stayed there two days. And many more believed because of His word. They said to the woman, "It is no longer because of what you said that we believe, for we have heard for ourselves, and we know that this is indeed the Savior of the world." (John 4:25–26, 39–42)

- *Jesus and the royal official shared this interaction—* Jesus said to him, "Unless you see signs and wonders you will not believe." The official said to Him, "Sir, come down before my child dies." Jesus said to him, "Go; your son will live." The man believed the word that Jesus spoke to him and went on his way. (John 4:48–50)

- *Jesus and the man born blind shared this interaction—* Having said these things, He spit on the ground and made mud with the saliva. Then He anointed the man's eyes with the mud and said to him, "Go, wash in the pool of Siloam" (which means Sent). So he went and washed and came back seeing. (John 9:6–7)

John's record of Jesus' words helps us understand the challenges Jesus faced. It was not the norm to receive Jesus at His word and grow up in Him. Jesus patiently called and, in the call, worked the trust He required. John recorded these interactions to help us see and believe that Jesus is patient as He calls us to grow and trust. Ponder these examples of branches of The Vine as they were challenged to grow and trust:

- *Jesus and Nicodemus shared this interaction—* This man came to Jesus by night and said to Him, "Rabbi, we know that You are a teacher come from God, for no one can do these signs that You do unless God is with him." Jesus answered him, "Truly, truly, I say to you, unless one is born again he cannot see the kingdom of God." Nicodemus said to Him, "How can a man be born when he is old? Can he enter a second time into his mother's womb and be born?" Jesus answered, "Truly, truly, I say to you, unless one is born of water and the Spirit, he cannot enter the kingdom of God. That which is born of the flesh is flesh, and that which is born of the Spirit is spirit. Do not marvel that I said to you, 'You must be born again.' The wind blows where it wishes, and you hear its sound, but you do not know where it comes from or where it goes. So it is with everyone who is born of the Spirit."

Nicodemus said to Him, "How can these things be?" Jesus answered him, "Are you the teacher of Israel and yet you do not understand these things? Truly, truly, I say to you, we speak of what we know, and bear witness to what we have seen, but you do not receive Our testimony." (John 3:2–11)

- *Jesus and Mary shared this interaction—*
  Martha said to Jesus, "Lord, if You had been here, my brother would not have died. But even now I know that whatever You ask from God, God will give You." Jesus said to her, "Your brother will rise again." Martha said to Him, "I know that he will rise again in the resurrection on the last day." Jesus said to her, "I am the resurrection and the life. Whoever believes in Me, though he die, yet shall he live, and everyone who lives and believes in Me shall never die. Do you believe this?" She said to Him, "Yes, Lord; I believe that You are the Christ, the Son of God, who is coming into the world." (John 11:21–27)

- *Jesus and Thomas shared this interaction—*
  Thomas said to Him, "Lord, we do not know where You are going. How can we know the way?" Jesus said to him, "I am the way, and the truth, and the life. No one comes to the

Father except through Me. If you had known Me, you would have known my Father also. From now on you do know Him and have seen Him." (John 14:5–7)

- *After Jesus' resurrection, Jesus shared this interaction with Thomas—*
Now Thomas, one of the Twelve, called the Twin, was not with them when Jesus came. So the other disciples told him, "We have seen the Lord." But he said to them, "Unless I see in His hands the mark of the nails, and place my finger into the mark of the nails, and place my hand into His side, I will never believe."

  Eight days later, His disciples were inside again, and Thomas was with them. Although the doors were locked, Jesus came and stood among them and said, "Peace be with you." Then He said to Thomas, "Put your finger here, and see My hands; and put out your hand, and place it in My side. Do not disbelieve, but believe." Thomas answered Him, "My Lord and my God!" Jesus said to him, "Have you believed because you have seen Me? Blessed are those who have not seen and yet have believed." (John 20:24–29)

- *Jesus and Philip shared this interaction—*
Philip said to him, "Lord, show us the Father, and it is enough for us." Jesus said to him, "Have I been with you so long, and you still do not know Me, Philip? Whoever has seen Me has seen the Father. How can you say, 'Show us the Father'? Do you not believe that I am in the Father and the Father is in Me? The words that I say to you I do not speak on My own authority, but the Father who dwells in Me does His works. Believe Me that I am in the Father and the Father is in Me, or else believe on account of the works themselves." (John 14:8–11)

The Vine identified those who were not in Him. He could see their hearts on their faces and in their actions. He said, "If anyone does not abide in Me he is thrown away like a branch and withers; and the branches are gathered, thrown into the fire, and burned" (John 15:6). The Vine faced His own sadness and anguish at the rejection He received because He knew that eternal life was found in His life alone.

We are called to be challenged by The Vine's words and actions toward people who would not receive Him. His words were harsh and unwavering, particularly toward the religious leaders who would not accept Him as The Vine that God brought up out of Egypt. His challenging words were a call and an opportunity to turn and be healed. Jesus quoted Isaiah and added words of blessing on the people for what they could hear and see:

> This is why I speak to them in parables, because seeing they do not see, and hearing they do not hear, nor do they understand. Indeed, in their case the prophecy of Isaiah is fulfilled that says:
>
> "You will indeed hear but never understand, and you will indeed see but never perceive." For this people's heart has grown dull, and with their ears they can barely hear, and their eyes they have closed, lest they should see with their eyes and hear with their ears and understand with their heart and turn, and I would heal them.
>
> But blessed are your eyes, for they see, and your ears, for they hear. For truly, I say to you, many prophets and righteous people longed to see what you see, and did not see it, and to hear what you hear, and did not hear it. (Matthew 13:13–17)

The Vine's work was to communicate His passion and love; His word challenges us to receive. He declares us alive and growing in Him, and His declaration provides the life it promises. He also says that in this world we will face trouble but that He has overcome the world. He assures us that His call, while challenging, is not a heavy burden. He says, "Come to Me, all who labor and are heavy laden, and I will give you rest. Take My yoke upon you, and learn from Me, for I am gentle and lowly in heart, and you will find rest for your souls. For My yoke is easy, and My burden is light" (Matthew 11:28–30).

We must not forget that Jesus faced the human challenges of hunger, fatigue, and temptation. Jesus chose to face the challenges of being falsely accused, mockery, a false trial, suffering, and death. He chose to step into those challenges for our sake so we know that He walks with us. He faced those challenges because He knew that they were the means through which God worked to bring every opportunity for forgiveness, life, and salvation to us.

The Branches Speak: The Apostles' Words

The apostles faced many challenges as they lived out their lives. They viewed extreme challenge as an opportunity to grow. It was while he was in the middle of his own challenges that Paul called believers to "give thanks in all circumstances." Please note that Paul did not call followers of Christ to give thanks *for* all circumstances.

As God worked in him and through him, Paul faced those challenges and didn't run from them. He gives us these powerful words to think about in light of the challenges we face as branches in The Vine:

- Finally, be strong in the Lord and in the strength of His might. Put on the whole armor of God, that you may be able to stand against the schemes of the devil. For we do not wrestle against flesh and blood, but against the rulers, against the authorities, against the cosmic powers over this present darkness, against the spiritual forces of evil in the heavenly places. Therefore take up the whole armor of God, that you may be able to withstand in the evil day, and having done all, to stand firm. Stand therefore, having fastened on the belt of truth, and having put on the breastplate of righteousness, and, as shoes for your feet, having put on the readiness given by the gospel of peace. In all circumstances take up the shield of faith, with which you can extinguish all the flaming darts of the evil one; and take the helmet of salvation, and the sword of the Spirit, which is the word of God. (Ephesians 6:10–17)

- For freedom Christ has set us free; stand firm therefore, and do not submit again to a yoke of slavery. (Galatians 5:1)

- We have spoken freely to you, Corinthians; our heart is wide open. You are not restricted by us, but you are restricted in your own affections. In return (I speak as to children) widen your hearts also. (2 Corinthians 6:11–13)

The apostle John faced many challenges as he lived in The Vine. Jesus called John and his brother James "the Sons of Thunder," for very good reason. They had the nerve to approach Jesus with evidence of their misunderstanding:

And James and John, the sons of Zebedee, came up to Him and said to Him, "Teacher, we want You to do for us whatever we ask of You." And He said to them, "What do you want Me to do for you?" And they said to Him, "Grant us to sit, one at Your right hand and one at Your left, in Your glory." Jesus said to them, "You do not know what you are asking. Are you able to drink the cup that I drink, or to be baptized with the baptism with which I am baptized?" And they said to Him, "We are able." And Jesus said to them, "The cup that I drink you will drink, and with the baptism with which I am baptized, you will be baptized, but to sit at My right hand or at My left is not Mine to grant, but it is for those for whom it has been prepared." And when the ten heard it, they began to be indignant at James and John. (Mark 10:35–41)

Mark calls us to ponder the challenges Jesus faced, especially with those He called to be His closest followers. Contemplate the difference between the disciples' request and response and the response blind Bartimaeus gave to the same question, "What do you want Me to do for you?"

And they came to Jericho. And as He was leaving Jericho with His disciples and a great crowd, Bartimaeus, a blind beggar, the son of Timaeus, was sitting by the roadside. And when he heard that it was Jesus of Nazareth, he began to cry out and say, "Jesus, Son of David, have mercy on me!" And many rebuked him, telling him to be silent. But he cried out all the more, "Son of David, have mercy on me!" And Jesus stopped and said, "Call him." And they called the blind man, saying to him, "Take heart. Get up; He is calling you." And throwing off his cloak, he sprang up and came to Jesus. And Jesus said to him, "What do you want Me to do for you?" And the blind man said to Him, "Rabbi, let me recover my sight." And Jesus said to him, "Go your way; your faith has made you well." And immediately he recovered his sight and followed Him on the way. (Mark 10:46–52)

The Gospel writers witnessed Jesus' word and work because they knew we would face challenges too. In spite of facing extreme challenges with followers who were selfish and stubborn, Jesus still says, "Ask anything in My name." He challenges us to receive that as an opportunity and to answer His question "What do you want Me to do for you?" John gave us these words that parallel Jesus' challenge and opportunity for us:

> Everyone who believes that Jesus is the Christ has been born of God, and everyone who loves the Father loves whoever has been born of Him. By this we know that we love the children of God, when we love God and obey His commandments. For this is the love of God, that we keep His commandments. And His commandments are not burdensome. For everyone who has been born of God overcomes the world. And this is the victory that has overcome the world—our faith. (1 John 5:1–4)

One of the greatest challenges of life in The Vine is receiving The True Vine at His word. It is so easy to mix things up. The apostles struggled with this challenge as they walked with Jesus, and we struggle with it too. At times we may get confused and think that it is our work instead of the work of The Vinedresser or The Vine. We may place burdens on other branches in The Vine or think it is our job to grow for them. We may think we can abide in The Vine without growing. We may choke ourselves off from the life-giving Vine as we spend our energy trying to bear fruit where it isn't our calling to bear fruit.

THE BRANCHES SPEAK: MY STORY

Challenges abound. We can ignore them, confront them, deal with them, accommodate them, or try to manipulate them. Challenges are in our face every moment of every day. We may be tired of challenges, tired of growing, or just tired. We may be blind to seeing challenges as opportunity. The vines speak two types of challenges: those we can control and those we cannot. In the vineyard, we address the challenges that we can control and adapt to those we can't.

I wanted to ignore or manipulate the challenges I faced. The Vinedresser called me to address that which was my calling to address and to adapt to what I could not control. The Vine kept me moving forward, and He kept me alive in His life. Growing was and is the only healthy option, and identifying challenges is part of the growing process. Part of the growing process is coming to the realization that challenges are opportunities to grow.

One challenge I needed to address was my "I'll do it myself," my "I can handle this situation on my own" attitude. I needed the help of others, but I had isolated myself. I kept pain and fear to myself. When I cried out, the people I cried out to for help were not equipped to help or even to comprehend what I was dealing with. They were not equipped to recommend professional help to me.

Another challenge I faced was the prevailing attitude I had grown up with: "If we don't talk about it, it will go away." As I grow up in The Vine, I'm realizing that many families choose to ignore or remain silent on hurtful issues. Silence leads to greater challenges of secrecy and isolation in painful circumstances. As I learned to admit the harm silence caused, challenge led to opportunity. I found my voice and, through that, I hope to give others the courage to find theirs. Challenging issues don't go away, even when we choose to ignore them or pretend they don't exist.

An additional challenge I faced was that over time, I began believing that I deserved to be treated poorly. I deduced that if I were better, I would be treated better. I believed I should put the best construction on everything. These and many other behaviors led to diminishing hope that change would come. I got used to a life of pain and silence. Even today, when I speak up, there is a twinge of guilt that I'm doing something wrong by saying I am hurting.

Another challenge I faced was "doing" because "being" was too painful. I worked to serve God and others. I taught and I believed. I longed for more because while I taught and I believed, I also doubted that God's mercy really was for me. A friend asked, "Why do you speak loudly when you teach?" She got to me. My tear-filled response was that I was trying to hear what I was saying. Challenging questions became powerful opportunities to grow.

Jesus' interactions with people often included profound questions. His questions challenged people and stimulated growth. I wrote down every question Jesus asked and was most profoundly affected by the account from Mark's Gospel mentioned above, "What do you want Me to do for you?" I meditated on how I would answer that question if Jesus stood before me. I was being challenged to think differently, to ask Jesus to do something for Me. I asked Him to open my heart to His word and work for me and in me.

I had been taught that the Law is a curb, a mirror, and a guide. I had been taught that I am a sinner in need of forgiveness and mercy. I had been taught that Jesus is the fulfillment of the Law, that He is my righteousness. I don't take issue with these teachings. I do have issues with some of the religious leaders who taught me. I had interpreted some of God's Word wrongly, and I didn't receive loving guidance in my interpretations. I was dying, and The Vine called me back to life in the words in John 15.

Jesus' words were full of life and mercy, but they didn't fall neatly into any categories. Growth took place through verses that challenged a narrow way of thinking about Jesus' word and work. Jesus said, "If you keep My commandments, you will abide in My love, just as I have kept My

Father's commandments and abide in His love. These things I have spoken to you, that My joy may be in you, and that your joy may be full" (John 15:10–11). I've pondered this question, time and time again: How can the commands make His joy and mine full if they are only a curb, a mirror, and a rule? John says the commands are not burdensome, and David declared that he loved the Law.

The vines spoke. The trellis system forms the structure of life (Law), which gives the branches freedom to grow and produce fruit. The "don't" God spoke in the garden was an opportunity to be free and worship Him. The Law *is* a curb, a mirror, and a guide, and that has so much meaning! God's "don't" is structure, and within that structure is opportunity for freedom to grow and bear fruit where we are called. Paul calls this a spiritual form of worship:

> I appeal to you therefore, brothers, by the mercies of God, to present your bodies as a living sacrifice, holy and acceptable to God, which is your spiritual worship. Do not be conformed to this world, but be transformed by the renewal of your mind, that by testing you may discern what is the will of God, what is good and acceptable and perfect. (Romans 12:1–2)

Another challenge I faced was acknowledging the scary distance that existed between my head (academic knowledge) and my heart (faith and trust). It was deep and wide. I had learned to play it safe. Only the sap dripping from The Vine kept me moving forward into the life God was calling me to grow into. Health, balance, and production are the goals of the vine; The Vine called me into the same. Health and balance in all areas of life (spiritual, emotional, physical) was the challenge and the opportunity to grow and bear fruit.

The challenges and opportunities were mine, and I was being called to grow through them. Part of growing up in The Vine included facing the fact that I was trying too hard (and unsuccessfully) to help my husband face his own challenges. I realized that I was being called to let go of the challenges that belonged to him. This challenge was a huge opportunity to develop healthy boundaries. The challenges I faced led to the opportunity to seek the help of a Christian mental health care professional. I was not equipped to face these challenges and grasp hold of the opportunities by myself.

I face challenges today as honestly and authentically as I know how. I know in my heart that Jesus' call always breeds growth and authenticity and honesty. My fears diminish as I learn to trust Christ's work in me and see challenges as opportunities.

THE BRANCHES SPEAK: YOUR STORY

The challenges you have faced in your past and are facing in your present are an important part of your story. God works through these challenges to bring you closer to Him. Your story is important and valuable, and God calls you to find your voice as He works in you and through you. Please take time to reflect and speak with your small group about your answers to the following questions:

1. What has The Vine spoken to you through this chapter on challenges and opportunities?
2. What challenges have you faced?
3. What have you learned from those challenges? Give examples of where you see more clearly how God has worked through challenging circumstances you have faced.
4. What opportunities do you see arising from the challenges you face today?
5. What word is The Vine speaking in your challenges today to help you see them as opportunities to grow?

Chapter Eleven

THE FRUIT OF THE VINE

THE VINE SPEAKS: MY FATHER'S VINEYARD

Our journey into the vine and the vineyards has brought us to the fruit. The vines speak their most profound message through the fruit they bear, and all the aspects discussed in previous chapters lead to the harvest. Quality fruit cannot result from poorly cared-for vines. Without the work throughout the seasons, the vines would not be healthy, and they could not bear quality fruit.

The flavors of wine grapes at the peak of ripeness are astounding and speak exactly what they are created to speak. At perfect ripeness, the grapes taste sweet but not too sweet. The flavors are bright and layered. The skins and the pulp have distinct textures and flavors as well. A tour of the vineyard is a sticky proposition as we pick ripe fruit clusters for our guest to sample.

We grow thirteen different wine grape varieties—five whites and eight reds—on our five-hundred-acre property. The white grape varieties include Chardonnay, Muscat Canelli, Sauvignon Blanc, Viognier, and Roussanne. The red grape varieties include Cabernet Sauvignon, Merlot, Zinfandel, Syrah, Petite Sirah, Barbera, Tinta Madera, and Touriga Nacional. The flavors of these different varieties are distinct and different, comparable to the difference between eating different varieties of apples, like Golden and Red Delicious.

Bearing mature, premium-quality fruit is our goal at Steinbeck Vineyards. Grapevines bear fruit naturally, but they don't bear premium fruit naturally, as we've discussed throughout this study. The vinedresser works year round with many hands-on touches to bring the best fruit from the vine. Making quality wine that will age properly requires both quality fruit and an excellent winemaker. Growing and selling premium fruit to our winery clients, including our own winery, is a year-round process.

The season's work culminates in a flurry of activity during harvest in September and October. We carefully and regularly check ripeness factors including sugar content, seed ripeness, acid balance, and color extraction from the skins. We taste the fruit, bite into the seeds to make sure they are a toasty, nutty flavor, and roll the skins on our fingertips to make sure color bleeds out. Winemakers or their representatives meet with us in the vineyard to assess the health of the vines during the final push.

Picking the fruit is scheduled with wineries a day or two in advance, giving us time to schedule trucks to haul the fruit to the processing plant. We schedule workers to pick the fruit. My family moves the tractors and trailers carrying large picking bins to the staging area so everything is ready when the workers arrive. Just before daybreak, workers gather, anxiously waiting to get started. When my father feels that there is enough light to pick, he gives the start command and the tractor drivers start the engines. The crews of five to eight people follow their tractor into the designated field.

The energy and excitement of harvest is focused on one cluster at a time as workers lift the branches to find the ripe fruit and quickly cut it off the vines with sharp knives. Thirty to forty pounds at a time are dumped into the large bins, which hold one or two thousand pounds. Each worker picks about two thousand pounds in one day, so if we need to deliver twenty tons to a winery, we schedule twenty people. If we need to pick fifty tons, we schedule fifty workers. During the picking season, we may pick five hundred tons of fruit by hand, which is about 25 percent of the fruit from our vineyard.

Most of our fruit is machine harvested. The fascinating, huge mechanical harvesters are towed behind our large tractors. The tractor travels the open row as the machine straddles the vines and gently shakes the trunk of the vine. The ripe fruit readily releases from the stems and falls into

A Harvest

buckets on a conveyor while the stems remain on the vine. Mechanical harvesting is efficient and desirable for large wineries, while handpicking is done for smaller wineries.

The year-long growing process culminates with picking the fruit. Mature fruit is delivered to our winery clients who then begin the amazing process of creating beautiful wine out of the fruit we've grown. We drink the mature wines one to three years after we've picked the fruit. A beautifully made red wine can age and become more complex for twenty to thirty years.

I am amazed at God's gift of the vine and the wine. I am also amazed at the life lessons the vine and vineyards provide. Ponder the progression of the life of the vine and the wine that the fruit becomes in terms of years. The newly planted vine takes three years to mature enough to produce its first crop. The fruit from that year, called the vintage, takes one to three years to be made into wine. The vine produces fruit annually for thirty to fifty years or more. Beautiful wine ages for twenty to thirty years or more.

My father and my son grow fruit on our thirty-one-year-old Cabernet vines that is crafted into beautiful wine by our winemaker. My son's son could enjoy wine crafted from the fruit of the vines that his great-grandfather, my dad, grew the year he was born. I pray that my father is still living and healthy twenty years from now so he can toast my grandson's twenty-first birthday with a glass of wine made from the 2011 vintage.

THE VINE SPEAKS: JESUS' WORDS

I am the true vine, and My Father is the vinedresser. Every branch in Me that does not bear fruit He takes away, and every branch that does bear fruit He prunes, that it may bear more fruit. Already you are clean because of the word that I have spoken to you. Abide in Me, and I in you. As the branch cannot bear fruit by itself, unless it abides in the vine, neither can you, unless you abide in Me. I am the vine; you are the branches. Whoever abides in Me and I in him, he it is that bears much fruit, for apart from Me you can do nothing. (John 15:1–5)

If you abide in Me, and My words abide in you, ask whatever you wish, and it will be done for you. By this My Father is glorified, that you bear much fruit and so prove to be My disciples. (John 15:7–8)

The Vine spoke: "You did not choose Me, but I chose you and appointed you that you should go and bear fruit and that your fruit should abide, so that whatever you ask the Father in My name, He may give it to you" (John 15:16). Different translations shed light on the word "abide" as it pertains to the fruit we produce. The New American Standard Bible says "that your fruit would remain," and the New International Version says "fruit that will last." The fruit of Jesus' life, the lives of the apostles, and the fruit we bear at His calling is fruit that will last.

The Vine's fruit was borne through His word and work. He spoke the Word and continues to speak! In the past, the Word spoke, and creation was the fruit of His work. Jesus, The Vine, spoke through His word and work as He walked this earth. His perfect life, His miracles and words, His suffering, death, and resurrection were, collectively, the fruit of His work. In the present, Jesus, The Vine, speaks through the Bible, and the fruit He bears is evident through His work in us and through us.

Jesus' earthly presence was a process of growing and being and living as a human being. The fruit of His life to which we pay so much attention was recorded in the Gospels so that we might believe. However, Jesus' whole life—His conception, birth, childhood, teen years, and adulthood—

worked toward the work He came to accomplish for us and in us. The perfect life of The Vine must be seen as a whole, like the life of the vine and the process of bearing fruit.

We have spent ten chapters unfolding the message of The Vine, and now we take time to explore Jesus' words about bearing fruit. We will proceed carefully as we discuss fruit in context, never straying from the abiding relationship we have as branches grafted in The Vine. The fruit He calls us to bear, the keeping of the commandments He calls us to keep, the loving He calls us to love, and the asking He calls us to ask all flow from the energy and life of The Vine.

The Vine spoke the words of John 13–15 to the disciples in the Upper Room just before His arrest and crucifixion. John records the purpose of Jesus' fruitful words: "to keep you from falling away" (John 16:1). In just hours, the disciples would witness the brutal crucifixion of their Lord and would be persecuted for following Him. Peter's denial and the flight of the others are examples of their response to the extreme conditions they faced as branches in The Vine.

John wrote his profound testimony of Jesus' word and work that we might believe and that believing, we have life in His name. The challenges we face as branches in The Vine in this world are significant, especially when coupled with our own fears of growing up in The Vine. Jesus' words call us to grow, and from this context, we listen as The Vine speaks about bearing fruit:

If you abide in Me, and My words abide in you, ask whatever you wish, and it will be done for you. By this My Father is glorified, that you bear much fruit and so prove to be My disciples. As the Father has loved Me, so have I loved you. Abide in My love. If you keep My commandments, you will abide in My love just as I have kept My Father's commandments and abide in His love. These things I have spoken to you, that My joy may be in you, and that your joy may be full.

This is My commandment, that you love one another as I have loved you. Greater love has no one than this, that someone lay down his life for his friends. You are My friends if you do what I command you. No longer do I call you servants, for the servant does not know what his master is doing; but I have called you friends, for all that I have heard from My Father I have made known to you. You did not choose Me, but I chose you and appointed you that you should go and bear fruit and that your fruit should abide, so that whatever you ask the Father in My name, He may give it to you. These things I command you, so that you will love one another. (John 15:7–17)

Jesus does not use the word if in the first five verses of chapter 15, only in verses 6–14. If we take these verses out of context, we might conclude that The Vine does His part and the branches do their part. If we think abiding and keeping are dependent on our work, we would have to believe Jesus contradicted Himself. If we take these words out of context, we would need to take a deep breath, roll up our sleeves, and work harder. We'd also need to rework the first ten chapters of this book!

But when we look at these verses in context, then we see that each "if" Jesus spoke, He answered. He answered the "if" in verse 7 with verses 8–9. The "if" in verse 10 is answered in verses 11–13. And He answered the "if" in verse 14 with verses 15–16. Please take time to process Jesus' answer to His own declaration "if." Jesus answers all of the "if" words and circumstances in our lives in His call to us to grow in His life and bear fruit.

We can be confident that when Jesus calls us into relationship with Him, He provides everything He demands. Jesus' accomplishment is the foundation of our relationship with Him and the context in which we bear fruit. We can also be confident that Jesus spoke these words about joy with the knowledge that He would soon glorify God through the fruit of obedience in the face of death on the cross. He declared, "These things I have spoken to you, that My joy may be in you, and that your joy may be full" (John 15:11). These are not words of a burden being placed on us, but words of freedom to be all He has created us to be and to bear beautiful fruit He has prepared for us to bear.

The word "glorified" in verse 8 warrants attention as we proceed with our study of bearing fruit. Jesus said, "If you abide in Me, and My words abide in you, ask whatever you wish, and it will be done for you. By this My Father is glorified, that you bear much fruit and so prove to be My disciples. As the Father has loved Me, so have I loved you. Abide in My love" (John 15:7–9). God is glorified when healthy branches of The Vine do what branches do: bear much mature fruit. The fruit we bear is proof, or manifestation, of the relationship we have in The Vine as His disciples.

Jesus regularly spoke the words "glorify" and "glorified." He used these words within the context of doing and completing the work He came to do. Through Jesus' word and work, God was glorified—that is, made manifest, or revealed. And, Jesus said, God is glorified by the fruit we bear—He is made manifest, revealed, through our work.

Here are some examples of The Vine's words about God being glorified in His Son and the Son being glorified through His work:

- But when Jesus heard [news of Lazarus's death] He said, "This illness does not lead to death. It is for the glory of God, so that the Son of God may be glorified through it." (John 11:4)

- "Now is My soul troubled. And what shall I say? 'Father, save Me from this hour'? But for this purpose I have come to this hour. Father, glorify Your name." Then a voice came from heaven: "I have glorified it, and I will glorify it again." (John 12:27–28)

- When [Judas] had gone out, Jesus said, "Now is the Son of Man glorified, and God is glorified in Him. If God is glorified in Him, God will also glorify Him in Himself, and glorify Him at once. Little children, yet a little while I am with you. You will seek Me, and just as I said to the Jews, so now I also say to you, 'Where I am going you cannot come.' A new commandment I give to you, that you love one another: just as I have loved you, you also are to love one another. By this all people will know that you are My disciples, if you have love for one another." (John 13:31–35)

- Whatever you ask in My name, this I will do, that the Father may be glorified in the Son. If you ask Me anything in My name, I will do it. (John 14:13–14)

- When the Spirit of truth comes, He will guide you into all the truth, for He will not speak on His own authority, but whatever He hears He will speak, and He will declare to you the things that are to come. He will glorify Me, for He will take what is mine and declare it to you. All that the Father has is mine; therefore I said that He will take what is mine and declare it to you. (John 16:13–15)

Each of these passages launches us deeply into abiding relationships. Jesus has an abiding relationship with the Father and the Spirit, the Father and Spirit have an abiding relationship with the Son, the Son has an abiding relationship with us, and we have an abiding relationship with the triune God. God made Himself manifest in the life of His Son; God glorified Himself in the life of His Son and the fruit He bore. God makes Himself manifest in the life He gives us; God is glorified in and through our lives as we bear fruit as branches in The Vine.

Shortly after Jesus said "I am the Vine" and before He moved out of the solitude with His disciples into the chaos of the dark night, He prayed. His High Priestly Prayer recorded in John 17 gives us a glimpse into the beautiful conversational prayers Jesus shared with His Father. In this passage, Jesus acknowledged that the accomplishment of His work on earth glorified His Father.

> When Jesus had spoken these words, He lifted up His eyes to heaven, and said, "Father, the hour has come; glorify Your Son that the Son may glorify You, since You have given Him authority over all flesh, to give eternal life to all whom You have given Him. And this is eternal life, that they know You the only true God, and Jesus Christ whom You have sent. I glorified You on earth, having accomplished the work that You gave Me to do. And now, Father, glorify Me in Your own presence with the glory that I had with You before the world existed.
>
> "I have manifested Your name to the people whom You gave Me out of the world. Yours they were, and You gave them to Me, and they have kept Your word. Now they know that everything that You have given Me is from You." (John 17:1–7)

Jesus' words from The Vine to the branches and from The Vine to The Vinedresser leave no room for dormant living. Jesus' words call us to grow. When we're stuck in the notion that we don't have energy for fruit bearing, He reminds us that our energy flows from His roots, His nutrients, and His life. If we're questioning our purpose in life, He calls us to receive the relationship He has established, and He nurtures and enables us to trust that God works through us for His glory.

If we think that eternal life is "someday," Jesus calls us to see with eyes of faith that eternity is knowing Him now, grafted into His holy life in the present. If we're searching for work to do for God, He calls us to look right in front of us to the work He has prepared in advance for us to do (Ephesians 2:10). If we're burned out by doing, God calls us to be *in* Christ. If we're lazy in self-centered focus, He calls us to look up and out, to focus on Him. As I said before, Jesus answers our "if" situations and challenges with a loud call to grow and bear fruit in Him.

Like life in the vineyard, our life in The Vine has seasons of rapid growth and seasons of rest. All work toward the goal of mature fruit. While the vinedresser tends to the vines, a beautiful aspect of watching plants grow is watching them do what they do, freely and naturally. Bearing fruit has no formula. One branch doesn't judge another or compare fruit. To some branches The Vine said, "Come with Me." To others The Vine said, "Stay home and tell what I've done in you, for you." He spoke most harshly to religious leaders who put a heavy burden on people and narrowed the scope of what fruit was acceptable.

One type of fruit people produced as they encountered Jesus was receiving and simply being in His presence. Another type was giving and serving. In Christ there are no quotas; we'll never know of some of the fruit we've borne. We don't take credit for the fruit we bear or brag about it because in The Vine, we bear fruit naturally. It's what we do. And in The Vine, we don't sell ourselves short, because He has called us to rise up to work through us. He makes our joy complete as we bear the fruit He has called us to bear.

Jesus' words to His disciples as recorded by Matthew give us pause to ponder Jesus' work through us. We are called to do the work right before us, often not glamorous, but necessary as we glorify God. God is manifested in us and to others through our work in this world: "Then the righteous will answer Him, saying, 'Lord, when did we see You hungry and feed You, or thirsty and give You drink? And when did we see You a stranger and welcome You, or naked and clothe You? And when did we see You sick or in prison and visit You?' And the King will answer them, 'Truly, I say to you, as you did it to one of the least of these My brothers, you did it to Me'" (Matthew 25:37–40).

Jesus, The Vine, is the best winemaker ever. The perfect wine, made from water and His Word, was served at the wedding banquet in Cana. The Vinedresser grafted us into the life of The Vine through water and the Word. The perfect wine is served as we feast on His body and blood for forgiveness, life, and salvation. The wine crafted of the fruit of our lives will last because that is the promise from The Vine. Jesus said, "You did not choose Me, but I chose you and appointed you that you should go and bear fruit and that your fruit should abide, so that whatever you ask the Father in My name, He may give it to you" (John 15:16).

THE BRANCHES SPEAK: THE APOSTLES' WORDS

The mature fruit God worked in and through the apostle Paul has been passed down through the generations. Paul's fruit weaves a rich tapestry of life in The Vine throughout his letters. These words from his letters are not new to us, but today they call us to grow in Christ in the context of being grafted into The Vine and bearing fruit as branches.

- God, being rich in mercy, because of the great love with which He loved us, even when we were dead in our trespasses, made us alive together with Christ—by grace you have been saved—and raised us up with Him and seated us with Him in the heavenly places in Christ Jesus, so that in the coming ages He might show the immeasurable riches of His grace in kindness toward us in Christ Jesus. For by grace you have been saved through faith. And this is not your own doing; it is the gift of God, not a result of works, so that no one may boast. For we are His workmanship, created in Christ Jesus for good works, which God prepared beforehand, that we should walk in them. (Ephesians 2:4–10)

- The fruit of the Spirit is love, joy, peace, patience, kindness, goodness, faithfulness, gentleness, self-control; against such things there is no law. And those who belong to Christ Jesus have crucified the flesh with its passions and desires. [The list of the desires of the flesh can be found in Galatians 5.]

  If we live by the Spirit, let us also keep in step with the Spirit. Let us not become conceited, provoking one another, envying one another. (Galatians 5:22–26)

The apostle John's fruit has been discussed throughout *The Vine Speaks* as we have studied his record of the words and work of Jesus. His letters called people—us—from darkness to light in the Son of God; from the ever-present twisting of the truth into the life of the Truth. Abiding, loving, keeping, and asking are the fruits to which John calls us in The Vine. They are relationship words from the context of abiding in—living life in—The Vine.

- My little children, I am writing these things to you so that you may not sin. But if anyone does sin, we have an advocate with the Father, Jesus Christ the righteous. He is the propitiation for our sins, and not for ours only but also for the sins of the whole world. And by this we know that we have come to know Him, if we keep His commandments.

Whoever says "I know Him" but does not keep His commandments is a liar, and the truth is not in him, but whoever keeps His word, in him truly the love of God is perfected.
By this we may know that we are in Him: whoever says he
abides in Him ought to walk in the same way in which He
walked. (1 John 2:1–6)

- Little children, let us not love in word or talk but in deed
  and in truth. By this we shall know that we are of the truth
  and reassure our heart before Him; for whenever our heart
  condemns us, God is greater than our heart, and He knows
  everything. Beloved, if our heart does not condemn us,
  we have confidence before God; and whatever we ask we
  receive from Him, because we keep His commandments and
  do what pleases Him. And this is His commandment, that
  we believe in the name of His Son Jesus Christ and love one
  another, just as He has commanded us. Whoever keeps His
  commandments abides in God, and God in Him. And by
  this we know that He abides in us, by the Spirit whom He
  has given us. (1 John 3:18–24)

- Everyone who believes that Jesus is the Christ has been born
  of God, and everyone who loves the Father loves whoever
  has been born of Him. By this we know that we love the
  children of God, when we love God and obey His commandments. For this is the love of God, that we keep His
  commandments. And His commandments are not burdensome. For everyone who has been born of God overcomes
  the world. And this is the victory that has overcome the
  world—our faith. Who is it that overcomes the world except
  the one who believes that Jesus is the Son of God? (1 John
  5:1–5)

THE BRANCHES SPEAK: MY STORY

My friend's husband died in a military helicopter crash when their daughter was six weeks old. Janine raised her daughter as a faithful single mom, together with the help of her parents. I sat with her the day the doctors gave her the news that she had just two weeks to live. She pinched her skin and with a half-smile and questioning eyes, she said, "I don't feel that dead yet." I listened as she expressed her awareness of her impending death. Our pastor consecrated the Lord's Supper. Janine, her family, and I shared Christ's body and blood. We talked about being grafted into The Vine, that we are alive in Christ as we live on this earth, that we live in Him now and after we die.

I sat at her bedside and held her close the day before she died of cancer. She asked me to pray, and so, with tears of sadness and joy, I prayed that God would give us courage and hope. I asked God to hold us and keep us in His everlasting care. I prayed for her sixteen-year-old daughter and for her parents who were saying good-bye to their dear daughter. I had no words to end our prayer, and so we lay together in silence and tears. When I gathered myself and calmed the lump in my throat enough to speak, I said, "Just know that Jesus is holding you." In a weak, tender voice, she said, "I know He is because you are."

The fruit of her life lives on through her daughter and through her last, very true words to me. We are Christ's hands and feet and heart and voice in this world. We did not choose Him; He chose us. He chooses to work in us, and He chooses to work through us. God worked through Jesus' fruit, through His word and work, to draw us to Him; God works through our circumstances to draw us to Him and through the fruit of our lives to draw others to Him.

We've grown so accustomed to and comfortable with believing that we need to be serving. Serving is beautiful fruit we bear. However, finding value and worth only by giving is a problem. We are uncomfortable when we are on the receiving end because we believe that having needs is a sign of weakness. Transactional living gets things done. Growing in The Vine and nurturing meaningful, healthy relationships must be process oriented. Growing vines is a process; life in The Vine is a process.

Our fast-paced, user, throw-away society breeds transactional living, and so many people are desperately hurting. Many people who are no longer able to give feel worthless because they found worth only in giving and serving. Our culture uses people, and the church also breeds a culture of using. I asked this question in previous chapters: Does our doing define our being, or does our being define our doing? The Church needs to be a safe haven where saying no is as okay as saying yes.

Modern language in Christian circles includes the phrase "God is using you." I take issue with that language. God is not a user; God is a work-througher. The Vine is not a user; The Vine is a work-througher. Jesus worked through the blindness of the man who could not see; Jesus worked through the death of Lazarus; Jesus worked through the cross and the grave. Jesus works through us as we bear fruit, and Jesus works through us as we receive the fruit others bear for us.

We are Jesus' hands and arms and feet and heart and voice in this world as He works through us. Those around us are His hands and arms and feet and heart and voice for us as He works through them. As we bear fruit as branches in The Vine, it is important to discern where we are called to bear fruit and where we are not called to bear fruit. Living in The Vine gives us freedom to grow and bear fruit where we are called and freedom to let go of work we are not called to do.

The journey from transactional to process living mirrors the journey of God's Word from my mind to my heart. Learning to trust the work of The Vine in me and through others for me has challenged me to grow and bear much fruit over these past years. The work of God in me from the context of the life of The Vine has shaped God's work through me. The work of The Vinedresser is never done as He works for us and in us and through us as we bear abiding, lasting fruit.

The Word of God clearly calls us to bear fruit that will abide. The Word of God calls us to walk in the good works He has prepared in advance for us to do. The holy callings to which we've been called might include changing diapers or cooking meals or driving children to school. We might be called to give from our heart financially or with our time in many and various ways. Giving in our homes is as high and holy a calling as giving in the Church. We may be called to bear the fruit by learning to say no. We may be called to bear the fruit of receiving.

Growing in The Vine produces the fruit of authenticity, transparency, and honesty. Growing produces the fruit of developing healthy boundaries: for example, realizing that the fruit you are called to bear isn't the same fruit I am called to bear gives us both opportunity to be the people God created us to be. For me, ending my marriage was necessary and fruitful. For you, working on your marriage is necessary and fruitful.

Branches in The Vine are unique and uniquely positioned to touch lives around them through bearing the fruit they've been called to bear. Growing in The Vine also encourages self-examination with a true desire for further growth and maturity. Living the fruit of repentance, the fruit of receiving mercy, and the fruit of giving mercy are profound examples of living in Christ's life.

The fruit of our vines will age to a well-made wine for generations. Generations who have gone before us bore lasting fruit, as is witnessed by the fruit of our faith. Our desire to study and grow and be faithful to God's Word as we allow it to work in us and through us has a fruitful history. The fruit we bear is a result of all of the hands-on care given by the

Vinedresser and The Vine. As branches grafted into The Vine's life, we live in His life now and for eternity. As branches grafted into The Vine's life, we bear fruit that will abide.

THE BRANCHES SPEAK: YOUR STORY

Fruit bearing comes naturally through life in The Vine. The Vinedresser and The Vine work to bring growth and good fruit through the branches. Each of us is called to ask God for discernment and courage and hope in all aspects of growing and bearing fruit in The Vine. The Vine's desire is that we abide, love, keep, and ask anything in His name. Please share with your group your answers to the following questions:

1. How has The Vine spoken to you through this chapter?
2. How do the following verses impact your "being and your doing"? "You did not choose Me, but I chose you and appointed you that you should go and bear fruit and that your fruit should abide, so that whatever you ask the Father in My name, He may give it to you. These things I command you, so that you will love one another" (John 15:16–17).
3. How do the following words of Jesus resonate with your experience of life in The Vine? "These things I have spoken to you, that My joy may be in you, and that your joy may be full" (John 15:11).
4. List places you are called to bear fruit. List areas where you may not be called to bear fruit.

CONCLUSION

Touring Steinbeck Vineyards in my rusty 1958 Willys Jeep is a beautiful, dusty, bumpy ride. Touring the Word of God through *The Vine Speaks* was a little like our vineyard tour. We could have stayed at an arm's length, but that would have been too easy. We dug down deep, and we'll continue on the journey—receiving, growing, and bearing fruit. May God bless your journey in The Vine.